FIND YOUR PLACE IN GOD'S MISSION

Jeremiah Gibbs

Find Your Place in God's Mission

The General Board of Higher Education and Ministry leads and serves The United Methodist Church in the recruitment, preparation, nurture, education, and support of Christian leaders—lay and clergy—for the work of making disciples of Jesus Christ for the transformation of the world. Its vision is that a new generation of Christian leaders will commit boldly to Jesus Christ and be characterized by intellectual excellence, moral integrity, spiritual courage, and holiness of heart and life. The General Board of Higher Education and Ministry of The United Methodist Church serves as an advocate for the intellectual life of the church. The Board's mission embodies the Wesleyan tradition of commitment to the education of laypersons and ordained persons by providing access to higher education for all persons.

Wesley's Foundery Books is named for the abandoned foundery that early followers of John Wesley transformed, which later became the cradle of London's Methodist movement.

Find Your Place in God's Mission

HIGHER EDUCATION & MINISTRY
General Board of Higher Education and Ministry
THE UNITED METHODIST CHURCH

CONTENTS

ACKNOWLEDGMENTS

Special thanks are due to the eight friends and colleagues who allowed their stories to become centerpieces of this book. Thanks to Michael Cartwright, Kory Vitangeli, and Lilly Endowment, Inc. for their ongoing support of the Lantz Center for Christian Vocations. Thanks to Audrey Foster and Payton Reingardt who read and provided excellent feedback on this book. Thanks to my wife and son for supporting me in my work on this and so much else.

WHAT AM I GOING TO DO WITH MY LIFE?

Well-meaning parents, teachers, and family friends frequently ask high school and college students: "What are you going to do with your life?" If you're part of a Christian community, then the question is often asked with a slight twist, something along the lines of "What is God calling you to do?" I've been asked this same question many times; so often, in fact, that I've come to believe the question, and attempts to answer it, won't go away no matter how old I get. When you're gathering for graduation parties or announcing your college choice, there is a lot of pressure to have an answer, and not having an answer can make you feel like you have somehow failed. It feels like you have no ambition or goals. So many of us just pick something to study . . . anything . . . because it feels better to have some answer, some sort of direction, than to have nothing. And who among us wants to lack direction? Yet, a hasty choice just increases our anxiety, because often uncertainty about our choice, made under pressure, remains.

1

At the heart of the "calling question" in Christian circles is a nasty assumption. Many believe that God has one thing that you are supposed to do—one thing—and if you miss it, you're out of luck. It's as if that calling is hidden deep in the recesses of heaven, and somehow you have to figure it out or risk missing God's plan for your entire life: "Find God's calling on your life and you will be fulfilled, happy, and prosperous. But if you don't hear from God and, instead, follow the wrong path, you will live outside of God's plan and God will be displeased with you." That is a lot of pressure placed on one decision. It's no wonder people get so nervous about it.

> God loves you and wants
> you to have a fulfilling life.

This nasty assumption is lousy for another reason, for what does such a belief say about God? God as revealed in Jesus Christ proclaims, "My yoke is easy and my burden is light" (Matt 11:30). Jesus isn't a God who places impossible decisions in our path. When I was young the video game systems would often have "cheat codes," which were long strings of particular button presses. "Up, Up, Down, Down, A, B, A, B, Select, Select, Start." If someone told you the secret code, then you had to work hard to be able to execute the code at the right time so that you could unlock the game's secrets. God's calling is far from the "cheat codes." Jesus is certainly not a God who hides his will for our lives and waits for us to make the right combination of choices that illuminates the true path. God is one who makes the path clear by revealing himself in Jesus, saying to his disciples, "Follow me." Following God is primarily about doing the things that clearly lead to a faithful life: offering kindness to our neighbor, striving for justice, practicing a lifestyle of prayer, and harboring a deep commitment to a worshipping community are just the beginning.

> We are called to live as disciples
> of Jesus and follow his direction.

You are called to live as a disciple of Jesus and follow his direction. This is the good news of Jesus Christ! You can know right now that this is what God is calling you to do. Never again do you need to anxiously wonder whether you have found God's path for your life. It is actually straightforward. Every person in the world shares this one calling. There is no figuring it out. You just have to do it. *You are called to live as a disciple of Jesus Christ.*

CALLED FOR A MISSION

Sometimes we try to reduce calling to a career or to the ways we will be involved in our church community: "I believe I am being called to start a small group at my church." But God's calling for each of us is to first and foremost live as a disciple. We don't just mill around aimlessly; we follow God's direction. That is what gives us direction and purpose—our mission.

God calls each of us to fulfill the mission. Most major theological traditions have wholistic definitions of discipleship. The
United Methodist Church describes its goal, its mission, this
way: to make disciples of Jesus Christ for the transformation
of the world. Being called to follow means we walk with others who are also called, who are also disciples. And we walk
so that others can enjoy the same benefits we do as the children of God, and join in. This is a great description, because
it names how we are supposed to be in relationship with God
as well as how we are to be in relationship with the world
around us. It calls us to proclaim the good news of Jesus and
to live a ministry of compassion.

> Following Jesus means we
> travel with other disciples who
> are also following Jesus.

OUR CALL BEGINS AT BAPTISM

God gave us this calling to discipleship at our baptism. The
liturgy of baptism is an excellent place to learn all that is en-
tailed in living faithfully as a disciple. Each denomination has
a slightly different liturgy for baptism, but most focus on a set
of core commitments that every Christian is called to live out.
The United Methodist Church frames baptism as an answer to
a set of four questions (found at the end of this chapter) that include promises and commitments we make to God, or, in the

case of infant baptism, are made on our behalf until we can decide for ourselves at confirmation.

First, we commit to repent of our sin. Repentance is not only a one-time moment in our spiritual walk but also a continual process of turning away from selfishness and actions and attitudes that lead us away from God and turning toward God. True repentance is accepting God's grace to live in faithfulness and putting God first. When we set our hearts to answer God's baptism call to repentance, we are committing to be in relationship with God, so that we can constantly and honestly evaluate our actions and inactions to know when we are not living in ways that are life-giving to ourselves and others.

We also commit ourselves to resisting evil and oppression wherever we find them. Pushing back the powers that keep others from their God-given life and health is one of the many ways that Christians can put God's story of redemption on display for the world to see. Although not every person is called to a career of justice work, every Christian is called to work for justice wherever they are.

At our baptism we confess that we will proclaim Jesus Christ as Savior of our lives and put our whole trust in his grace. As we proclaim Christ as Lord of our lives, we are saying that we will put our wants and hopes at the foot of Jesus's cross and let him change our hopes and desires to the ways of God's Kingdom. We are trusting that God's grace is enough, even for our failures.

The fourth baptismal vow is a promise to serve faithfully in our church and to be faithful in our service for the mission to the world. Many people today act as if the church is like a basketball game or a counseling service. If they really want to hear a good message and enjoy some music, they will wake up early on Sunday morning or maybe go on Saturday night and view the service as something to enjoy as they would a sporting event. If their life is a mess and they need help navigating tough choices, they will go talk with their pastor. Both of those things are good, and I wouldn't want to discourage either. But our baptismal calling requires more than engaging in the life of the church only when it is pleasurable and helpful to us. The Church is God's primary way of working out the Kingdom mission of Jesus, so that all can have a fulfilling life. We make promises to be part of that mission, so we have a responsibility to support the life of the Church with our prayers, presence, gifts, service, and witness.

ALL CHRISTIANS ARE CALLED

I know what you are thinking. "So what? That is all good and well, but it doesn't help me know what job I'm supposed to pursue." Actually it does, but let's start a step before that. Jesus taught his disciples to pray "your kingdom come, your will be done, on earth as it is in heaven." That little bit of the Lord's Prayer is at the center of the hope of the Church. We are a people who are praying for the realities of this present world to line up with the way things are in God's realm.

Scripture offers no greater vision of this than the last chapters of the Bible where the book of Revelation explains the New Heaven and New Earth as a place where "there will be no more death or mourning or crying or pain" (21:4). The New Heaven and New Earth is described as a place where there will be no temple, which was the place where God was believed to be most present for the original audience of Revelation. There will no longer be any need for a temple, because God's dwelling place will be among the people (Rev 21:1-4). But this isn't the reality that we experience as we observe our world today. Famine, abuse, hunger, and war are the norm. Broken families often mean growing up without a mom or dad or growing up in two homes and juggling time between them. Friends and leaders cannot always be trusted, because suspicion tells us that any one of them may be willing to use us for their own benefit. We experience the realities of a broken world nearly every day in relationships that are stressed by selfishness, competition, deception, and an always increasing pressure to prove that we are good enough.

What are committed people of God to do with this? How do we live the call of the Lord's Prayer for God's Kingdom to come "on earth as it is in heaven" when the realities of this world are so far from heavenly?

In the Gospels, the seventy-two disciples Jesus sent out in groups of two were merely ordinary people who needed to be instructed as to how to act and what to do: "When you enter a town and are welcomed, eat what is offered to you. Heal the sick who are there and tell them, 'The kingdom of God has come near to you'" (Luke 10:8-9). Jesus understood healing, teaching, and proclamation to be ordinary ministry. And he knew that because they represented him—God present in the flesh—the Kingdom of God would be present. Our task as Christians in mission is to enter into relationships with our neighbors and enact the heavenly kind of world, that is to be Jesus's hands and feet. This makes us all ministers (see 1 Pet 2:5). This is ministry for not just the world but for us as well. Even though a world without mourning, death, crying, or pain will not be fully realized until Jesus comes back in power, the mission of Christians is to live out, embody, that heavenly reality now.

outside

> Wherever you do the work of the Kingdom, you are doing the ministry of the Church.

Jesus told the disciples to proclaim, "The kingdom of God has come near to you." Jesus might have been referring to himself, but he was also surely referring to the Kingdom of God becoming present through the ministry of the disciples. How great is that? We, together, are on a mission to be living examples of the Kingdom of God coming to the places around us. Wherever we do that, we are doing the work of the Kingdom of God—and we have entered into the ministry of the Church.

None of this tells us what job we as individual disciples are supposed to do with our lives, however. Obviously no one person can carry the weight of every ministry of the Church. Such a task will require all of us. When we talk about "finding our calling," we don't typically mean finding this big and broad definition of calling that I have been describing. This broad definition is often referred to as the *general calling* of every Christian. The *general calling* of every Christian is to live a life of discipleship. When we talk about finding God's calling, we usually mean that we want to know God's *particular calling* on our individual lives. *Particular calling* is a phrase that theologians use to describe the way that a particular person uses their unique passions and abilities to fulfill God's mission around them. Every Christian's particular calling is just a narrow aspect of this general calling of all Christians. Let me explain what that means.

OUR PARTICULAR CALLINGS

I understand my ministry as a teacher and theologian to be one aspect of my denomination's mission to faith formation or what we typically call "discipleship." It's easy to see how that is a narrower aspect of the big, broad mission of the Christian life. But what about the accountants of the world? What about the music teachers? How does God call someone to be a farmer? Is a calling to restaurant management really an aspect of Christian mission? Each of these professions pertains to an aspect of God's overarching mission for every Christian, but sometimes we struggle to understand how until we have been trained to see it.

Two examples can make my point: the accountant's primary aims are efficiency and accountability. If an accountant does his or her job well, then management can make good decisions about how many workers they will need to complete a particular job. A good accountant is also responsible for detecting when people have used money and other resources poorly or if they have stolen from those resources. If the accountant does this aspect of the job well, then they can prevent fraud or theft. By doing so they contribute to what The United Methodist Church's baptismal vows call "resisting evil." By keeping people honest, the accountant helps to prevent theft from creating greater brokenness and distrust between people. People around them can begin to get a sense for what heaven will be like when all greed and theft will be destroyed in the New Creation. And when the accountant is able to help the company operate efficiently and manage their resources well, it means that this business will continue to be able to operate according to its mission, which in many cases will also contribute to the making of a better world. Even when the work itself may be driven more for profit than for the good of all, the accountant helps that business manage itself efficiently and therefore keeps people in their jobs and able to feed their families.

Recently I had a role in making a decision that we knew would cost lots of people their jobs if we chose incorrectly, and there was a tremendous sense of responsibility that helping people stay employed was a good in itself. This is part of the mission of an accountant, and it is a good and holy calling. The world needs honest and upright accountants. In one way we could say that it is part of every Christian's calling to help the world have less theft and fewer people without jobs. If a Christian has an opportunity to stop someone from stealing, they have a call, a mission, to do so. Or if they have a chance to help someone get or keep a job, they should do so. A Christian accountant is one who specializes in witnessing to God's coming Kingdom in these ways.

The music teacher also has lots of opportunities to form faithful persons. Two of these are particularly important. First of all, all Christian discipleship is primarily learned by practice. Becoming proficient in Christian practices can be like practicing a musical instrument. A person cannot learn to play an instrument in the abstract, by reading about it or watching YouTube. To become a musician you have to play regularly and often. You learn by doing. If a person wants to become a more faithful follower of Jesus, it requires, for example, prayer each day, regular study of the Bible, offering compassion to those who are in need, and showing mercy to friends, family, and colleagues who make mistakes. Music is learned the same way as religious faithfulness. Each day a musician must practice their scales and exercises. They have to listen to great music and put in the time to painstakingly learn to re-create the work of the masters. So when students learn to be disciplined in repetitive practice of music, they learn one of the central ways that they will also grow close to Jesus through constant attention to prayer, scripture, worship, and so on.

Music teachers also enable students to understand the importance of beauty and learn to know it when they see or hear it. Learning to see beauty is essential to learning to see the beauty of the Gospel and the Christian life, which at first glance may not seem too beautiful. Long-time Christians may miss this point, but I'm glad to remind you that our good news starts with rebellion, generations of suffering and disobedience, and the killing of our God. So a person who reads the Bible story may be tempted to believe that it is not good news. But what if the ability to perceive music's complexity, harmony, and resolution actually teaches us to learn to appreciate those as aspects of the Christian Gospel? When we learn to see beauty in one place, we will have a greater ability to perceive it in other places. We seek it out, and when a music teacher helps a student learn how to practice in a disciplined way and teaches that student to appreciate a beautiful composition, they may in fact be preparing a student for the most critical skills needed to live a mature Christian life. That's one small aspect of the broad and overarching call of Christian discipleship and mission that is fulfilled by teaching music.

We *could* work through many more examples, but my point should be clear. We might say that a calling is a person's discipleship specialization. All callings to specific careers are simply a commitment to a single aspect of the overarching call upon every Christian. There may be some careers that a Christian will not be called to serve. Many people are surprised to learn that early Christians were not permitted to be bankers, actors, or soldiers. Bankers committed the sin of usury, lending money at extreme interest. The Greek word for actor was *hypocrite*, because actors were presenting something other than their true selves. And Christians were forbidden from killing, even while serving as a soldier. Yet most Christians now consider each of these careers to be an important calling from God. Christians in every age will have to ask what careers are forbidden for people of faith, but the overwhelming majority of careers that a modern person of faith may pursue can be a calling to a life of discipleship and mission.

Knowing that many careers can enable us to live God's mission does not resolve the difficult questions about how to discern one's career calling. But it does give us a path to discovering it. If you want to discover God's particular call upon your life, you must be engaged with God's mission for the world. Proclaim the Gospel. Resist evil. Show compassion to the sick and destitute. Set the captives free. In the midst of one of these callings that we all share is the particular calling that God has for you.

As I said above, this is really a necessary prelude to hearing God's voice specifically for your life. But since it's *necessary*, you don't get to skip this step. The first and most important step for every Christian who is discerning, trying to figure out, God's calling is to move forward in their faithfulness and answer God's call to discipleship.

HOW CAN THIS BOOK HELP ME FIND MY CALLING?

Find Your Place in God's Mission is about a discernment process. Discernment means that you carefully listen and evaluate, so that you can take your next steps. Discernment is always a judgment call, so it pays to seek wisdom—your own and that of others. And the process suggested in this book is one that you can use for the rest of your life to continuously take steps of faith and follow where God is taking you next. Whether you are a young person preparing for university and your career, or you are much older and changing career or finding a new mission for your retired life, every stage of life requires that you spend time discerning what God would have you do next. My hope is that this book will teach you a simple process that you can use for the rest of your life to make decisions about what you should be pursuing next.

Discernment means that you carefully listen and evaluate, so that you can take next steps.

Sometimes it helps to have a roadmap to where we are going before we start a journey. Let me give you a quick overview of where we will be going in this book. Chapter 2 is going to look at some of the key scripture texts about calling to help us understand how the Bible can be a relevant resource. Many people spend too much time looking around for burning bushes or angel messengers, because they haven't had a chance to think through the scripture passages well. We will explore what to do if we hear one of these powerful and miraculous callings and how to know if what we have heard was indeed God's calling. In chapter 3 we will learn the organizing framework for discerning our calling. This chapter will ask you to begin an inventory that can be used as you read the rest of this book. That framework will be summarized in one sentence: God's calling is found where your *passions* intersect with your *tools* at the point of the *world's needs*. I'll explain why these three—our passions, our tools, and the world's needs—are so critical to your calling. Much of the book after this point will then help us take an inventory of how each of these three are present in our lives. Chapter 4 will focus on the *world's needs* and define these in terms of our theological commitments. The Bible and our faith help us to see what the world most needs. Chapter 5 will focus on understanding our *passions* and how passions will fuel our work and calling when things are most difficult. Chapters 6, 7, and 8 will help us to explore various aspects of our *tools*.

Rather than just evaluating what we are good at, we will also consider the unique ways that God has made us and our experiences and how that helps us to minister to God's world. Chapter 9 will help us see how to use all this information that we have been gathering about ourselves. We will practice using that information to consider some possible callings that we could pursue. Chapter 10 is for those considering professional ministry in the church. While God calls people to all kinds of careers, I am aware that this process of discernment may make many begin to consider whether God is calling them to be a pastor, youth minister, missionary, or one of many other kinds of professional ministry. The last chapter will help you begin to figure out if this particular calling may be God's plan for your life.

Now that you know where you are going, get ready for a powerful process of discernment. The discernment process is powerful because it asks you to put the lordship of Christ at the center of your decision making. Even before you begin to do the work God has called you to, this time of discernment will grow you spiritually as you ask Jesus to be Lord of your life. Be open to how God will push you to put God's will first in your decisions. Take some time to pray for that openness and growth before you consider the discernment exercise below.

DISCERNMENT EXERCISE

The questions that are asked of baptismal candidates are a good summary of what it means to respond faithfully to the call to Christian discipleship.

1. Do you renounce the spiritual forces of wickedness, reject the evil powers of this world, and repent of your sin?

2. Do you accept the freedom and power God gives you to resist evil, injustice, and oppression in whatever forms they present themselves?

3. Do you confess Jesus Christ as Savior, put your whole trust

15

in his grace, and promise to serve him as your Lord, in union with the Church, which Christ has opened to people of all ages, nations, and races?

4. According to the grace given to you, will you remain a faithful member of Christ's holy Church and serve as Christ's representative in the world?

Take a moment to write down the ways that you are living each of these commitments in your life right now. Then go through each question again and write down some practical things you could do to live each of these commitments better.

GOD'S WILL IS NOT A SECRET

In chapter 1, I suggested that many conversations about Christian calling assume that God's calling is a secret that must be uncovered. When I hear people talk about calling, it often sounds like they are suggesting that God has one specific career that they are supposed to do, one person to marry, one college to attend . . . you get the idea. It is as though the goal is to figure out the one specific path God has for their life. Their concern seems to be that if they get too far off this path, they might miss God's best for them.

I imagine this perspective of God's will to be a little like the giant corn mazes that are common in the Midwest. There are so many turns between the entrance and the exit that you will almost certainly make a few wrong choices. And some of those wrong choices may leave you wandering in the maze for hours with no idea how to correct your path. These can be a fun adventure with friends when you know that someone will eventually come rescue you if you can never find your way out. But if we are talking about our lives—career, marriage, children, and so on—then the consequences of getting lost in the "calling maze" of pursuing God's will can be pretty scary. Most of the conversations that I have with high school and college students about their future and choices have an assumption like this behind them. Rarely does anyone question whether this is how God's will works. Usually I just hear more questions about how to make better choices on the calling maze or how to know if you have made a correct choice. But I believe this notion of God's calling is wrong for most people.

There are stories of God's calling in the Bible. While these stories may seem that God had one specific calling for that one specific person, remember that these stories were written in hindsight. Their endings were not prescripted; the plot lines are not straightforward, and each of the protagonists also made choices that took them off God's preferred path. That is part of the Bible's beauty, and there is always plenty of intrigue.

The prophet Samuel picks David above all his more qualified brothers. Moses sees a bush that burns but is not consumed and God, through the bush, tells Moses to go free the people. Paul has a miraculous vision of a man from Macedonia, and that comes only after a vision of Jesus knocks him down, resulting in temporary blindness. In each of these cases, God gives a specific task to someone. But looking at the details of these stories will help us see the pattern.

In 1 Samuel 15 and 16, the Lord rejects Saul as king and tasks Samuel with finding and anointing the new king. When he arrives, David isn't out praying about what God would do with his life. He is tending to the sheep, his calling from God up to that time. Samuel comes to David's family, then rejects the other brothers and asks for David's father to send for his youngest son—David. The Lord speaks and tells Samuel to anoint David as king, which he does. It takes some time after that for David to come into his role as king, but David never has to wonder what God wants him to do with his life. He only has to believe God's calling and be faithful to pursuing what is before him.

Moses has a miraculous calling in Exodus 3, and again the task before him is clear. Like David, Moses is going about his normal calling of tending a flock of sheep. As he does his work, God interrupts that routine and speaks to Moses from a burning bush to say, "So now, go. I am sending you to Pharaoh to bring my people the Israelites out of Egypt" (v. 10). The task is clear, but Moses has to learn first to live into the calling faithfully. True, Moses is reluctant at first, but God equips him and rids him of all excuses. Moses isn't fuzzy about the mission God has for him. And he isn't spending long hours in prayer discerning whether or not leading the people out of Egypt is God's plan for him. Moses only objects that he isn't well qualified for what God has called him to do. I will explain in chapter 7 how Moses was uniquely equipped for this calling, and how this initial resistance to God's calling is a common feeling. But notice that Moses knows what he is to do; he is just fearful of what obedience demands.

Paul has an experience as he is pursuing God's calling to preach to the Gentiles. Paul and his companions are pursuing their missionary calling to preach throughout the world. Acts 16 says that Paul "tried to enter Bithynia, but the Spirit of Jesus would not allow them to" (v. 7). We don't know how the Spirit prevented them from pursuing that path, but it must've been clear to them since they didn't seem to doubt it. Then Paul has a vision in the middle of the night of a man from Macedonia calling him to "Come over to Macedonia and help us" (v. 9). This is another instance of people going about their everyday tasks of life and God intervening to give them a clear vision of what is next for their life. None of these persons need to doubt what they are supposed to do, and none of them are said to be actively praying for discernment when this calling comes.

Many of the great call stories of scripture are similar. Abraham is called to leave his home (Genesis 12). Jeremiah is called to be a prophet (Jeremiah 1). Samuel himself is called by God by a still small voice in the night (1 Samuel 3). Mary is told by an angel that she will give birth to God's anointed (Luke 1). The disciples are busy fishing when Jesus invites them to join his mission (Matthew 4). Mary Magdalene and the other Mary are attending to burial responsibilities when Jesus makes them the apostles of the resurrection (Matthew 28). Perhaps we should be more surprised that these stories of calling do not come during times of prayer for God's direction.

If faithful people are intended to spend time praying about what they should do to follow God, we would think that scripture would have at least a few stories of people who prayed in this way and gained direction for their lives and calling. God does sometimes speak into a person's time of prayer and give them a vision for what they should do with their lives. Acts 10 has two examples of this kind of vision. The reference to Cornelius's vision "at about three in the afternoon" (v. 3) is probably an illusion to a time of afternoon prayer that demonstrates that he is a devout and God-fearing man. And God meets him in that prayer with a vision of Peter's arrival. Later in that story, Peter, too, is praying in the afternoon when he has a vision of God calling him to violate the cleanliness laws regarding food. Both Peter and Cornelius get clear visions from God while they are praying. But there is nothing to indicate that these prayer times are dedicated to discerning God's will in any way. In fact, the story is told to indicate that God intervenes in their rather mundane daily prayer practices. They are submitting to their everyday practices of devotion for the purpose of spiritual growth, and God introduces a specific and life-changing vision.

We are tempted to make these extraordinary stories the norm for Christian calling. Recently a student told me that she very much wants this kind of vision from God, because she wants to know what she should do, even if God's calling turns out to be incredibly difficult. Having the clarity about a specific thing is something she would welcome, so she knows what to do with her life to please God. But notice what happens in these Bible stories. When God has something specific for someone to do, God makes the voice that comes to them so blatantly obvious that not following it is to be clearly disobedient. Burning bushes. Prophets. Miraculous visions and dreams. I think these stories are in the Bible for one simple reason: the human authors that God used to write the Bible knew that these stories involved an unusual move of God.

(God calls us in different ways.)

DIRECT AND MISSIONAL CALLINGS

Theologian Doug Koskela (check out his great book *Calling and Clarity*) makes a helpful distinction between these miraculous stories of calling and the normal ways that God calls people into God's mission. He begins at the same place I did in chapter 1, with a distinction between God's "general calling" to discipleship and God's "particular calling" upon any individual Christian. But Koskela further distinguishes between two different kinds of particular callings: direct calling and missional calling. A *direct calling* is God speaking to an individual about a specific thing that person should do that may or may not be discernible from the normal practices of vocational discernment. All of the miraculous stories mentioned above are direct callings, but direct callings may also include the Spirit prompting a person to say something difficult to help a friend or make a financial gift that is particularly challenging. God can call people to do anything that God wants by these direct callings. These are very specific things God is calling them to do, and the only question is whether a person will be obedient to the clear calling that is before them.

Koskela says that God's *missional calling* is the invitation to join God's work in the world with your unique tools and passions, which can only be discerned by a prayerful process that often takes considerable time. Missional calling isn't a single task but a need in the world that you have been gifted and impassioned to give your life to serve. Missional calling, like all callings, starts by living faithfully into the kind of life scripture demands of the faithful. Romans 12 is great guidance for

22

us. Paul tells us that if we will live holy lives and allow God to transform our minds, then we can know God's will for us. According to Paul, following God's will is a moral matter. I normally don't need a divine intervention to know what God is calling me to do. Do I speak grace to my friend that has experienced moral failure or do I speak the truth in love? Is there some combination of the two? In a situation like this, Paul says that if you allow God to renew your heart then you will know what is a truly righteous response. If you live a holy life that is connected with the needs of your community, there may be any number of ways in which you can join God's mission. There is great freedom here to pursue those aspects of God's mission for which you are passionate and gifted to make a difference. God doesn't normally tell you one specific place that you are supposed to join God's mission, because there isn't just one way that is good and holy. Any place that God is working, you are invited to join God in the work.

Does that mean that God has no plan for your life? No. God is sovereign, and God has a plan for you. God's sovereignty means that God is mysteriously working out his plan for us and all creation in ways that baffle our understanding. God has a plan for you, but it is not your job to figure out that plan and execute it yourself. God has your future under control without your assistance. Don't try to figure out what specific thing God has for you; just learn how to live faithfully. God will make sure that you are on the path God has for you if you act according to the call of God in the Bible.

All this means that there is no secret plan for your life that you have to figure out. This idea can be pretty jarring for those who are busy trying to navigate the calling maze to find the one thing they are supposed to do. So how is a person to make these decisions? I still believe adamantly that God can and does speak directly to people today to tell them what to do. I think the first thing to do is to offer a prayer to God and ask for that kind of specific direction. Maybe you will have a dream or meet a talking donkey—for that story, see Numbers 22:21-39. But if that kind of clear word of God does not come to you, then you must begin a discernment process. The first question in that process must always be about what is most in line with a Christian way of life and ethic. According to God's Word, what is the moral thing to do?

Note

> Don't try to figure out what God has for you; just live faithfully. You can trust God. That is enough.

CHOOSING GOD'S WAY

Sometimes we aren't trying to decide between a moral option and an immoral one. Those who are trying to pursue God's will are rarely considering between one blatantly sinful option and one good option. If you are making that kind of choice, then God's calling is obvious. Sometimes we have several options before us, and each is a morally good choice. When we have exhausted the moral questions without a conclusion, these are normally matters of freedom.

Most of the time, however, we are making decisions between multiple *good* choices. In those cases, decide what is best and then act. That doesn't mean God doesn't care what you decide; it means God is more concerned with how you make the choice than the actual choice that you make. When we are faced with two good choices, God wants to see us choose in ways that honor the mission God has for us and honors the people impacted by the decision. The process of discernment by which we make the decision is an act of faithful discipleship. It matters very much for our faith. But God is sovereign and will accomplish God's mission in the world no matter what we choose to pursue. So you can have confidence that the choices you make will not take you outside of God's will for your life, as long as they are consistent with scripture and what we know of God's moral will for our lives. God's moral will is not a secret that God has hidden and can only be revealed by the Spirit. God's will has already been revealed through the incarnation of Jesus and the gift of scripture. Pursuing God's calling means obedience to what God has already revealed.

If following God's calling is about the particular ways that we are passionate and empowered to live out discipleship, then it should be obvious that calling is not only about the kind of work we will do. The most common calling questions I hear from young people are about the work they will pursue. Questions about who God is calling me to marry and where I am supposed to live and who I am supposed to befriend are much rarer. But each of these aspects of calling are just as significant as where we will work in God's mission. Calling is about living every aspect of your life in line with God's command to faithful discipleship. Work is just one piece of that calling.

GOD'S CALLING CAN BE LIVED IN DIFFERENT WAYS

While that is entirely true, much of this book will focus on questions of where we will spend our lives for the sake of God's mission. Even with that way of pursuing calling, you still have to think about more than just your job. For example, if God calls a person to the missional calling of helping people with disabilities to live a fuller life, this will work itself out in many different ways. They may find work as an occupational therapist. At church they may develop a means for the deaf to receive closed captioning in worship or lead a campaign to make the church building compliant with the Americans with Disabilities Act. They may also begin to bring the mail in for their elderly neighbor who is having trouble walking. This calling to serve those with disabilities isn't just about a job but about many ways that they will serve in God's mission. Discovering this aspect of calling is the primary purpose of this book.

Pursuing God's calling is even broader than discovering one's missional calling. God's calling will give you direction for whom you marry, whether to have children, where to live, how much to spend on your house or car, and so many other aspects of your life. These are all just as important as the way you will work in God's mission. But I focus this book on discerning your missional calling for a very practical reason: this is the area of calling where most people—especially the young people with whom I work most closely—are already most actively considering God's call. Many who are reading this already have the sense that they need to discern where they can make a difference in the world with their work. So these decisions take front and center in this book. But the good news is that the method of discerning calling that you will learn here, with regard to your work, is the same method you will use to discern calling in every area of your life. That method of discerning calling is the primary idea of chapter 3.

DISCERNMENT EXERCISE

Take some time to read some of the miraculous call stories in scripture (listed below). How many people do you know who have experienced stories like these? If most people do not experience such miraculous stories, then maybe God's calling on our lives is not so limited either.

- Abraham (Gen 12:1-5)
- Moses (Exod 3:1-12)
- Ruth (Ruth 1:15-18)
- Samuel (1 Sam 3:1-10)
- David (1 Sam 16:6-13)
- Esther (Esth 4:9-17)
- Jeremiah (Jer 1:4-19)
- Jesus lives into his calling (Matt 3:13–4:25)
- Mary Magdalene and the other Mary (Matt 28:1-10)
- Mary, Jesus's mother (Luke 1:26-38)
- Samaritan woman (John 4:1-30)
- Philip and the Ethiopian eunuch (Acts 8:26-40)
- Lydia (Acts 16:11-15)
- Timothy (1 Tim 4:6-16)

THE
INTERSECTION
OF CALLING

When Anna Palmer graduated from Harvard Law School, she had opportunity to become a highly paid lawyer. However, her creativity and commitment to Christ were leading her a different direction. Watching church rummage sales as a child reminded her that people's unwanted stuff could be worth money if sold to the right buyer, and folks were often willing to donate things they don't need. Consequently, she started the Fashion Project as a way that people could donate expensive designer clothing and the sale of that item would be donated to the charities of their choice. It was meaningful work because they were able to empower charities to do the good work they were already doing all over the world. Anna says that her life mission is to help people who are at a disadvantage to get access to opportunity. The Fashion Project was her starting place, but her commitment looked different when she started her next initiative.

Through her early work she realized that women founders were at a terrible disadvantage in gaining access to capital to start their companies. So she started two companies to empower women founders. JoinDough.com helps people to "shop like a wallet feminist" by highlighting consumer products from women-owned companies. The sales generated are a boost to the companies and help them get the attention of investors. But she also joined together with other women founders to create a venture capital firm to fund women-owned businesses as well. Both projects are creating opportunities for the next generation of women founders, a group that has historically gotten less than 3 percent of venture capital investments. Anna saw the disadvantage that women founders faced, and she created companies that make opportunities for those women. It gives her life purpose, and she is passionate about the community she serves.

Anna says that she has two talents that have been critical to her success at this work. First, she is able to see connections between things that other people don't. Her experiences of church rummage sales and seeing Goodwill's successful model of soliciting donations connected with the unique opportunity to utilize this model with designer fashion. Others hadn't recognized the opportunity that Goodwill and others missed by selling these designer items for a fraction of their value. Anna's other great talent is the ability to get people to commit to the ideas that she was pitching to them. She had learned to influence them through her authenticity and passion, and others are willing to trust her with their effort and their money. Seeing connections and the ability to convince others to join her have led her to amazing opportunities in just her first ten years of work. For the next thirty years, she plans to use these talents to create opportunities for disadvantaged people in lots of other spaces.

God's specific calling on a person's life is always a smaller piece of God's overarching call to witness to God's coming Kingdom. God has initiated a giant plan of redeeming the whole world and remaking it into a "new heaven and a new earth" (Rev. 21:1), where there will be no more death or mourning or crying or pain. The mission of the Church is to become the kind of community that will show the whole world how God's coming Kingdom will look. This will include all kinds of ministry to one another that will require we forgive one another, be gracious to one another, and hold one another accountable to a faithful way of life. This will also include ministry with and for the world that brings healing to the hurting, release and comfort to the prisoner, and abundant life to those who live under oppression. If the Church fails to witness to the coming Kingdom of God in any way, then a part of that heavenly vision is lost for all those who need to see it. But that doesn't mean that each Christian is called to live out every aspect of God's mission in the same way.

> Every Christian is called to prayer; worship; giving time, talent, and resources; fellowship; and study.

Every Christian is called to prayer; worship; giving time, talent, and resources; fellowship; and study. Every Christian is called to act justly and serve the needs of those around them. We are called to live every aspect of the life devoted to faithful service to God. But we all will also become specialists in a few of those areas of God's calling. As I explained in chapter 1, this is our particular calling within God's overarching general calling. The particular missional calling of every Christian is to dedicate their life to one aspect of the general calling to discipleship and become the Church's leading edge of ministry in that area. Not every Christian is called to empower women to start businesses like Anna. But she is leading all of us in thinking about how we can help women who are at a distinct disadvantage to men who start companies. We aren't all called to be leaders in the same areas of faithfulness. The real question we are asking as we discern God's calling for our life is "What aspect of God's mission is my specialty?"

Here is what I sometimes jokingly refer to as the "formula" for discovering God's call: God is calling you to the place where your *tools* intersect with your *passions* at the point of the *world's need*. I use this image of a map to illustrate how this works.

The X's on the map represent the *needs of the world*. Of course, these needs are geographically all over the world, but they also represent all kinds of needs. When a teacher pours him- or herself into a troubled teen or conservationists save a species from near extinction, the good news of God's Kingdom is proclaimed. And those needs are found in rural Indiana, urban Detroit, and Nairobi. As we will see in the next chapter, it is important that we pursue a calling that meets needs in the world because this is what will give our lives purpose and

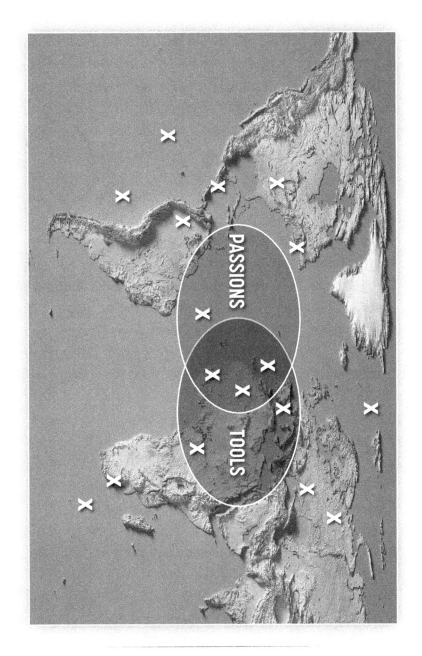

Discernment Map

meaning. We all want our lives to matter, and we will know that they matter as we participate in God's mission in the world. When Anna lays her head on her pillow each night, she has a sense of purpose that she has contributed to God's mission of improving the lives of people at a disadvantage.

One circle on the map represents your unique *passions*. These are the things you really love and also the things that make you really angry. The reality is that no matter what you spend your life doing, there are going to be times when doing it will be difficult. In those moments you are going to have to be so overwhelmingly committed to what you are doing that you can push through the hard times. Your passions will be what makes it possible for you to keep going when you are most ready to quit pursuing your calling. For Anna, that passion comes from seeing the impact she is able to make on people's lives. It keeps her going when things are challenging.

The other circle on the map represents your *tools*. Even if you are passionate about some needs of the world, if you have nothing to offer then it isn't your calling. If all that you have is a hammer, then you can't fix the plumbing no matter how hard you try. But all of us have some tools; we just need to take inventory of them so that we know what we have to offer the world in service. Our tools include our personality, experiences, gifts and talents, and resources. I will discuss each of these later in the book, as well as give some methods and practices to help discern these different tools. Anna is a great example of this because her great talents to see connections between things and to get people to join her in the work may not seem like tangible skills. But she has used those two traits to make huge impact on people's lives.

Here is where you get to the heart of discerning your calling. God's calling for you is found in the overlap between those two circles on the map. One of those X's *in the overlap* is God's calling for your life. We spend a lifetime discerning what's contained in the circle and what is outside of it. It won't be easy to discover, but it isn't a secret. Discover your passions. Take inventory of your tools. Become aware of needs in the world. Your calling will be where those three come together, and they will likely come together in multiple ways.

You will notice that the map has some needs of the world that are not within your passions or your tools. The body of Christ has a diverse mission and others will be called to meet those needs. Some needs of the world are within your passions but not within your tools. Some needs are within your tools but not within your passions. We will learn how to think about each of these in later chapters. You will also notice that there are multiple needs within your passions and your tools. As we will see, even after you have discerned your possible callings there will still be several good options open to you.

As you discern God's calling, you may sometimes be tempted to be satisfied with only one or two of these aspects of calling. You may find a need that you are really good at helping fix but have no passion for. You may think to yourself, "This is important work and it pays my bills." But if you aren't passionate about it, then you will never be able to push through the miserable or monotonous days. Similarly, you may really love doing something and know that you are good at it, but if you are never able to see how it makes a difference in the world then your work will lack purpose and meaning. Work that ignites your passions and gives you a sense of purpose will still require you to discover how you will be able to contribute to the work with your set of skills and experiences. We have to learn enough about ourselves and the world around us that we can discern how God is using all three of these areas to shape our calling.

PRACTICES OF DISCERNMENT

Many people seek the quick and clear calling from God that comes with burning bushes and visions from heaven. We have already seen that these are extraordinary means of being given a direct calling from God. For most people, and in most situations, we have to follow the longer and more careful process of discerning God's calling on our life. It may be easy to see this as an inconvenient necessity that we have to endure. But these processes of discernment have the potential to be one of the greatest times of discipleship in our entire lives. We are going to pay special attention to prayer and community in ways that we rarely do, and we will be motivated to do so because we know that these decisions will have a big impact on our lives. Don't be anxious about the process but lean into faith in the God who has a wonderful plan for your life in ministry.

PRAYER

One of the most important practices for your vocational discernment will be to cultivate a life of prayer. Prayer is important for spiritual growth for many reasons, but some of those reasons are specific to your vocational discernment. Regular prayer will teach you to discern the voice of God speaking among the multitude of voices that will want to influence your career choices. You need to have the confidence of knowing which voices are those that lead you toward greater faith, and this comes through consistently listening for God's direction in everyday choices in the life of faith. Regular prayer will also be the place where you will willfully set your own desires aside as you ask God to be Lord of your life. Following God's calling on your life will rarely mean pursuing a career that you don't want to pursue; however, it may mean that you have to set aside some career choices that you would otherwise really want to pursue. A life of prayer is preparation for setting our own will aside to pursue God's will for our life. If you have not already cultivated a life of prayer, then your period of discernment is a great motivation to develop this discipline in your life.

CONVERSATIONS WITH MENTORS

Another critical aspect of discernment will be conversations with several mentors from your church, family, work, and school. I've found that many people, especially teens and young adults, struggle to be able to see their strengths and even their passions in their true light. It is tempting to listen to the voices of competition and comparison that would make us believe that we have little to offer. "I can't talk in front of groups the way that she can"; or, "I'm not nearly as good at math as he is." Discerning our gifts can be especially hard for young people who don't know their own strengths well. The voice of wise mentors can help us to see ourselves for who we are, with all of our true strengths and shortcomings. A good mentor will notice when you are most passionate and committed. They will see areas where you have special insight or skill. But to truly benefit from their perspective on your life, you will have to ask these people to speak into your discernment process. Several of the discernment exercises in this book are going to push you to discuss your tools and passions with a mentor. These are a great entry point into a longer conversation where you ask mentors to speak into your life. Many church leaders, coaches, and family members would be excited to talk about what they see in you, so have the courage to ask them for that feedback, and learn to trust them when they tell you what they see.

When looking for mentors, it is important that the person be someone you believe to be mature and trustworthy and that has your best interest at heart. If someone has a history of treating you or others with disrespect or has ulterior motives, then simply don't choose that person as a mentor. That maturity and trustworthiness will be the foundation upon which you can make yourself vulnerable to them and have confidence that what they observe in you is true. If they are wise, then you will also want to hear their advice as you make crucial life decisions.

SERVICE

There may be no more critical practice for vocational discernment than service to the Church and the world. Passion for a need in the world is most often developed by understanding what is wrong and what is at stake if healing does not come in that situation. We intuitively know this already because we all know someone who went away on a short-term mission experience or volunteered in a ministry at church and discovered God's calling on their life while serving there.

You may serve with your church's Vacation Bible School (VBS) program and realize you love teaching children when it had previously intimidated you. Another person may visit a clinic while serving in a developing nation and recognize the impact a nurse can have on the life of a hurting person. Frequently when we are serving in developing nations or in impoverished areas of our own town, we discover aspects of justice we had not understood previously. Christian service can be an outstanding way to discover a need and a passion that you can contribute to in meaningful ways. But service is also a great way to test the callings you believe you are being called to pursue. One of the most frequent things we do in the university is help students find an internship in the field they are considering, or something closely aligned with it.

When a student has a chance to engage in service similar to what they are discerning, sometimes they find that this work wasn't what they thought and decide to go another direction. But many people who begin serving in the field grow to love the people and work, and they are able to see up close the kind of impact they would be able to make. This practice of service becomes transformative as all three aspects of calling—tools, passions, and needs of the world—are enhanced and brought into clearer focus. As you discern God's calling on your life, find a place to serve in the area you are considering. If you don't have any ideas on where you want to serve, just serve somewhere, because being there will expose you to all kinds of needs that you never knew existed. I'm sure that when Anna served at her church's rummage sale as a child, she didn't know she was learning an idea that would eventually lead to starting a company that raised money for thousands of charities.

STUDY

The fourth practice I highly recommend for vocational discernment is study of scripture and theology. If our task as disciples is to witness to the coming Kingdom of God, then we have to know what the Kingdom looks like and especially in the area of ministry God is calling us to serve. Reading and careful study of the scriptures about God's Kingdom and the specific ministry you are considering will give you a vision of how God's will looks in that arena. To go a little further, I also recommend studying the works of Christian theologians on that topic. Some people think they can begin reading the Bible on their own and understand a topic without the help of those who dedicate their life to this kind of study. While we all should read the Bible for ourselves, we should also study those who have dedicated their lives to understanding scripture and theology.

PUBLIC WORSHIP

The final practice that I suggest for the journey of discernment is the public gathering of worship. While we should study on our own and pray on our own, public worship is a key supportive practice that enables the other practices. Preaching will cover a multitude of topics over time, exposing you to aspects of calling and making you aware of service needs and opportunities that you haven't considered. Gathering with other believers will provide opportunities to develop critical mentoring relationships. Practicing prayer and listening to the voice of God in a public gathering will teach you the proper ways to engage prayer on your own. Scripture calls us to not forsake gathering together (Heb 10:25), because public worship is the place where we are called back to faithfulness on a regular basis, so we do not get too far off the path of faithfulness.

All of the practices that I recommend here are really just the things that we need to do to become more faithful Christians. When we recognize that our particular calling is really just a specialization in one aspect of the broader call to Christian discipleship, it should be no surprise that the things we need to discover our calling are all just ways of becoming a more faithful follower of Jesus. Follow Jesus more closely and pay attention to these three key areas of your mission (your passions, your tools, and the world's needs) and you will discover God's calling for your life. The process of discerning that calling will be a great motivation for doing the acts of faithfulness that all Christians should be doing for their personal growth.

DISCERNMENT EXERCISE

Start your inventory. If you are trying to discern what God has called you to—whether in work, volunteerism, or church—this is a good time to start an inventory of the three areas discussed in this chapter: your passions, your tools, and the needs of the world. On a sheet of paper or poster board, make an inventory of these three areas.

If you are really a creative type, then maybe you want to create your inventory as a map. Draw those two large overlapping circles on a map but leave it blank except for the words *passions* and *tools* in each circle. As you discover things that fit in each circle for you, write them in the circle to begin a list. As you discover needs in the world, you can draw an X and label it with a need.

You can also print the vocation inventory available at JeremiahGibbs.com/Explore-Calling.

NEEDS
OF THE WORLD

Jenna McElroy's family is deeply committed to spending time together, whether it is making music as the church worship band or bird watching on a Saturday afternoon hike. When she was young, they cultivated a love for science and a commitment to mission. Her younger sister would eventually pursue a calling as a medical doctor, and Jenna thought that may be her calling too. When she never became settled with the idea of being a doctor, she eventually decided to earn a graduate degree in environmental science without being sure what job it would lead her to pursue. After graduation she looked for work doing research for the Department of Natural Resources, but eventually she was hired at a job close to her husband's work as an assistant manager for a city ornithology center. They care for a number of injured raptors and use the birds to educate the community about the impact of pollution and how to be good stewards of the earth. When Jenna first started, she saw her teaching gifts developing and saw that she could make a difference in the ways that people thought about nature. People's lives were better when they took time to appreciate nature and take better care of the earth.

As part of her job, she took a few training sessions on how they could create a less stressful environment for the birds. She had always loved animals, and she was finding a way that she could improve the lives of these birds that were doing an important work in education. Her passion for science came rushing back as she poured over articles on the application of animal behavioral sciences. She wasn't creating research in her job, but she was applying research to improve the health of the animals she cared for and empowering the work of education. She had long known that she was passionate about science and animals, and her life had always been about service. Now she was able to put all of these together to contribute to making a better world.

Much of the confusion about God's calling, as discussed in the previous chapters, comes from a misunderstanding of God's mission. Most Christians understand the ways that pastors, missionaries, and other professional ministers are fulfilling God's mission. God is using them to further the work of the Church in the world, especially preaching, worship, compassion, and discipleship. Many Christians can also identify the ways that all Christians are called to personal witness and evangelism. For example, I frequently hear people say, "God will use me to witness to my coworkers and help bring them to faith in Jesus." This idea of calling is the same as the calling on professional ministers but limited to the kinds of preaching and witness that all Christians are called to do. This kind of witness is part of the calling of every Christian, but calling goes much deeper than that.

> Every Christian is called to act
> justly and serve the needs
> of those around them.

Christians from more prophetic traditions of the faith claim that God's mission is primarily about the ways the Church serves those in need. In these traditions of Christianity, it is not uncommon to discuss the ways the Church is bettering the lives of others, and that alone is counted as fulfilling God's mission in the world. These Christians can sometimes fail to see the importance of teaching the good news or calling persons to faith in Jesus. Many Christians from both perspectives can sometimes narrow the scope of God's mission in the world much too far.

One of the great riches of the Wesleyan tradition of United Methodism is the commitment to keeping "social holiness and vital piety" together as requirements of God's mission in the world. Social holiness is God's command to every Christian to extend love to their neighbor in practical ways. Social holiness also requires that Christians do no harm to others, whether it is through what they buy, how they organize communities, or how they steward the earth's resources. Vital piety requires that we nurture our love of God. This includes keeping the spiritual disciplines of faith such as prayer, witness, worship, fasting, giving, and compassion. Vital piety also requires that Christians "go on to perfection" in the fruit of the Spirit: love, joy, peace, patience, kindness, goodness, faithfulness, gentleness, and self-control (see Gal 5:22-23). To "go on to perfection" is a Wesleyan way of challenging every believer to live, with God's gracious help, an increasingly holy life. It rarely means that we do everything exactly right, but we can have motives and intentions that are made holy by God's grace. The calling to hold social holiness and vital piety together as requirements of our faith is one of the great gifts of the Wesleyan tradition. There is a close parallel in the Great Commandment to love God and love our neighbor (Matt 22:25-30).

I think most people understand what it means to be called to be a missionary of the Church, which is how calling is often used in common language. Another sense of calling involves ways that people are called to serve others. It's not unusual for people to talk about feeling called to be a nurse or teacher or social worker. But I think even those who can find language to talk about calling for this broader group will often still struggle to make sense of how people like Jenna are contributing to God's mission in the world. Does taking care of birds and helping people care for nature have any impact on God's mission in the world?

The most important feature in understanding God's mission in the world is an understanding of where this world is going. If we know where the world is going, then we can discern the role that Christians are called to play in God's mission to make that new world. When we read scripture, we see only glimpses of how the New Heaven and New Earth will look, but we know that God is remaking the world into a place where "there will be no more death or mourning or crying or pain" and where the presence of God will be among the people and God will dwell with them (Rev 21:3-4). The

New Heaven and New Earth is described as a place without suffering or injustice, and relationships between humanity and God as well as within the human community are without sin, competition, and suffering. This radical vision of God's healing creation and humanity is a promise for which we all long.

Jesus proclaimed, in both his ministry and life, that we can see the Kingdom of God coming near to us. Jesus was the "firstfruits" of that promised coming Kingdom (1 Cor 15:23). So even though we look around and see a world that is suffering the consequences of sin, we can know that the promises of heaven are also available to us now. We can't experience them fully yet, but we can get a foretaste of God's promises when we experience intimacy with God in prayer and worship. We also get a foretaste of heaven when we enter into communities that have learned to love one another well and are actively working out their salvation by their kindness and care for one another. When we experience that kind of worship and community, we can know that we are experiencing a little bit of heaven.

We can experience a foretaste
of God's Kingdom now.

I often think about the foretaste of heaven in the same way that I experience dinner being slow cooked in my kitchen. I can smell the aromas in the air, and I know that something good is coming just a little later. Anticipation builds as my hunger increases for the promise that is coming. And then there is a moment when I sense that it is getting close to being ready. I grab a spoon and dip it into the Crockpot or pan to get just a small sample. That small taste affirms what I have been hoping and makes me even more confident of what is ahead. It also increases my hunger and anticipation. I think this is what it's like when we come to the table of Holy Communion or experience baptism and confirmation in the faith. The same can be said of those holy moments that we experience true and genuine friendship and connection. Each of these moments gives us a taste of the holy, and they make us desire God's Kingdom in greater ways.

Christians are not the ones who build the Kingdom of God. God does that work through the power of the Holy Spirit. But Christians are the ones who proclaim the Kingdom of God to the world, and they only have the ability to proclaim the coming Kingdom if they are living it out in their own lives of discipleship. Each time a Christian acts with compassion toward their neighbor, they show the world what the Kingdom of God is like. Each time we gather for worship, we welcome people to encounter the presence of God among us. When we offer the table of the Communion meal, we allow people to experience a place where there is room enough for all with a main course of unrelenting grace. Others can experience forgiveness, dedicated service, true joy, and so much more of the Kingdom of God when the people of God live into the heavenly vision. In this way, Christians are those who distribute that little taste of the promised meal. We are the ones who offer a taste of the Kingdom so that others will grow in their desire for the whole of the promise.

We will often come up short of this heavenly vision. While God is sanctifying us, helping us to align more closely with God's image and purposes, God isn't finished with us yet. We will continue to sin, and we will never fully embody the heavenly vision that is depicted in scripture. To carry the analogy a little further, the taste of the dinner that isn't ready yet also doesn't quite taste right yet. But it is close enough that we can get excited about what is coming. Every moment of triumph and proclamation of God's coming Kingdom will be followed by a moment of failure because of our sins or the sins of our brothers and sisters in the faith. Part of the Wesleyan vision of sanctification is that Christians must go on toward the heavenly vision of the world as we are sanctified by God's grace. This is how we empower our own witness as we live that heavenly vision well.

Because we are called to participate in God's mission by sharing a taste of heaven, we can also begin to understand how all the various work we do in the world can be an aspect of the general calling to faithfulness that we share. How can those people who don't work in the church every day witness to God's Kingdom in the way I have mentioned? The best way to think about this is through some specific callings that people may have on their lives.

Imagine a person who has been called to work as a nurse or a doctor. When they help a person come into a better life and experience physical health, they participate in the healing that is promised for all. A person who experiences that healing can know that God is active in their journey. Those who work in a ministry of healing show the world about the coming Kingdom where they will receive complete healing.

It's just as easy to see how a teacher or social worker may be able to witness to the Kingdom. The teacher can help persons become healthy and whole members of the community, able to contribute to God's mission in the world themselves. Similarly, the social worker or the counselor helps people escape destructive patterns in their lives and relationships. While the professionals in these fields may not be able to publicly acknowledge this as a goal of their profession, social workers and counselors are really "sin destroyers," as they can help others to live in healthier ways. It is easy to understand how these human service callings can contribute to the witness to God's coming Kingdom. These people help end suffering, pain, and death. And the New Heaven and New Earth is a place where suffering doesn't exist. When people experience healing under the ministry of one of these persons, they experience a taste of the Kingdom of God.

It can be a little more difficult to think of how some other careers help people experience the Kingdom. In chapter 2 I described the work of an accountant who stamps out corruption. This helps to prevent sin from damaging others. We can all be honest and ethical. We can all encourage greater financial health. This helps a business keep and pay employees who can then feed their families and live well.

Looking back on the work that Jenna does each day, we can see that she is showing people a relationship with the earth that is more like the stewardship calling that God intended for humans. When we read Genesis 1, we see that God intended for humans to care for the earth and all its plants and animals as stewards, trusted caregivers. Even though humans have often gotten that wrong, some of the descriptions of creation indicate that God is busy healing the earth just as God is healing humanity. The New Heaven and New Earth isn't just about a renewed humanity but the restoration of the earth God has given us.

When Jenna helps people have better relationships with nature, she is restoring the desire to be good stewards that God intended for us. The birds that she cares for are largely injured because of pollution and other human interferences. When Jenna works to create the best environment that she can for the birds, she is restoring them to a place of greater health and less conflict with humanity. She is witnessing to God's coming Kingdom of peace by restoring peace to these animals.

One final example to make this point. I have often heard people contrast "meaningful work" with jobs such as factory worker or trash collector, as if those jobs contribute to God's mission in lesser ways. Imagine a person who assembles cars in a factory. We may be tempted to think that this job has little to do with the Kingdom of God and begin to criticize how much money the company makes or does not make for the shareholders. I've heard people say: "I don't want to work so that some rich person gets richer; I want to work for the Kingdom of God." But this misses an important aspect of the work of assembling cars. When I got in my car this morning, I needed the car to start when I turned the key so that I could go to work and get my son to school. And when I pushed the brake pedal on the interstate, I needed to know that the car would stop before crashing into the car in front of me and risking the safety of my family and the family in the other car. If the people assembling my car were not careful about their work, I may not have gotten to work safely. I might have been at the side of a hospital bed praying that my son lives, or I may not have gotten to work where I had important conversations with students about their faith and life. Because my car was assembled well by a trustworthy person, I was able to avoid death and suffering and enabled to contribute to the healing of the world. If the factory worker did that work well and efficiently, then the company has a better chance to be profitable and provide income for their coworkers and families. Workers in manufacturing, no matter the section—construction equipment, electronics, or other—are able to provide safety and efficiency to people's lives so that they can live into the fullest and best kinds of lives.

As I mentioned in chapter 1, Christians in every age must discern which jobs are not consistent with Christian calling. The Early Church decided that the military, for example, was not a Christian calling in their time, while today we honor this as a calling from God. Recently I questioned whether Christians can participate in the payday loan industry or work for "buy here, pay here" car sales. Both of these charge exorbitantly high interest rates that often take advantage of poor people, saying they are just poor credit risks. However, many poor persons, who cannot otherwise borrow to pay their bills, still need a car to get to work. While there are faithful people working in television and movie industries, telling stories that inspire and challenge, it's safe to say that Christians should not be involved in making and distributing pornography. Faithful people probably cannot work for tabloids that only seek to uncover "dirt" on celebrities for the sake of entertainment and ruining lives, but Christians will find good work in journalism that defends dignity and exposes injustice. I certainly don't intend this as a comprehensive list, but just a few suggestions of how to think about careers that Christians should not consider as faithful to God's mission.

We all want our lives to matter.

As I mentioned in chapter 3, there is one important reason why we must all pursue work that contributes to God's mission in the world. All of us want our lives to matter. When we are able to make a significant difference in the world, we get a sense of purpose from what we do each day. Jenna loves that she can improve the lives of the birds she has grown to love. And she loves that she can help urban children who don't often experience nature to understand that everyday choices to reduce pollution are important. My life is more meaningful when I have an important conversation with someone that helps us both grow closer to Jesus. Those are just a few examples of how pursuing God's mission in the world will give you a sense of purpose for your life.

DISCERNMENT EXERCISE

Spend some time browsing the internet looking at websites that talk about needs that are dear to your heart. Don't just look up those needs that we all know about like hunger and homelessness. Learn about the need for teachers in the inner city, the need for scientific solutions to fuel shortages, and the shortage of basic health care domestically and internationally.

If you can't think of anything, just search for "greatest needs in . . . (a city/country, business industry, etc.)" or "injustices in . . ."

The internet exercise is a good place to start. If you really want to understand the world's needs, you need to engage in the practice of compassion for those who have been in need for many years. Serve in soup kitchens and talk with the guests. Travel to a region (domestic or international) that is in great need. Go to a church in the worst area of your town and ask the pastor or some members what the needs are in their area. Volunteer at your local park or animal shelter. Talk to a scientist about what problems they are trying to solve with their work. To get a sense for the needs in your area, you need to get to know some of those needs through personal research. You may even just pose a question to your social media contacts: "What do you think are the greatest needs in the world today?" We can learn a lot from those who are closer to people's needs than we are.

Any needs in the world that you discover can be recorded on the "needs" section of your inventory. At this point you should record them on your inventory even if they are only vaguely interesting to you.

FIVE

PASSIONS: ANGER AND LOVE

As a young girl, Hannah Bast and her family went to a church in an area plagued with poverty. For a young person in a middle-class family, her church's ministry to their neighbors gave her a heart to serve those who live in poverty and led her to study social work in college. Each of her early internships and jobs were meaningful in different ways, but she still wasn't quite settled in her first job after graduation. While working elsewhere, she began volunteering at Back on My Feet. Hannah had been a competitive distance runner in college and had kept up her regular runs after her competitive career had ended. Back on My Feet is a national organization that combats homelessness through the power of running, community support, and essential employment and housing resources.

Hannah decided to volunteer with Back on My Feet so that she could keep up her regular running and to set an example of volunteerism for the outreach group she led at her church. The connection between the homeless population that she loved to serve and her passion for running was great for her. It wasn't long before a position opened for a workforce development coordinator, helping members of the organization build job skills and find employment. While her passion for running was a significant part of what led her to the job, she discovered an even more significant passion for the work shortly after she was hired.

Previous work she had done had upheld a fairly significant boundary between clients and professionals. They frequently talked about serving the whole person, but rarely did professionals build the depth of relationships that allowed them to help every aspect of a client's needs. Back on My Feet encouraged more in-depth relationships with members through the regular practice of running together, a time when the relationship was less formal than when they were limited to meetings in the office. She knew that this was how she most wanted to engage the people she served, and her love for Back on My Feet's approach grew. The percentage of persons who return to homelessness or succumb to addiction is incredibly high. And there are plenty of days when she is discouraged by the progress among those she serves. But the depth of relationships she is able to build with them allows her to thank God for the weeks or months when they are living a better life. And thankfully this wholistic approach is also very effective for her homeless friends because they have a community that they have built through running together. The activity—daily runs and walks—is a means to an end. But this activity leads to relationship, and both the running and the relationships are two of Hannah's greatest passions.

Frederick Buechner famously said, "The place God calls you to is the place where your deep gladness and the world's deep hunger meet" (*Wishful Thinking: A Seeker's ABC*). I think Buechner was missing a key component in discerning God's calling (your "tools"), but his insight that our passions are central to understanding God's call on our life is crucial.

WHY PASSIONS ARE IMPORTANT

Why are our passions so important? The theological answer is that God instilled these passions within us. Sometimes God sparks these passions in us in a moment, and sometimes God ignites passions in us over weeks or years of experience. But we can trust that they come from God's good plan for our lives. And we often need God's help in order to act wisely on our passions. God created all of us with an innate desire for all that is good. N. T. Wright, in his book *Simply Christian*, claims that we all desire beauty, justice, relationships with people, and a relationship with God. That list seems like a good starting place to suggest that we all have these four universal desires, but we don't desire them all equally. We may all desire justice for those who are hurting, but others of us may be more drawn to communication with God (prayer) than we are to freeing those who are enslaved. Our tendency is to imagine one of these desires as more righteous or fundamental than the others. But our desire for justice, beauty, and relationships is no less a desire for God than the desire for prayer. Ministry to the oppressed is no more central than creating that which is beautiful. God puts particular passions within us that we might commit to one aspect of the variety of Christian callings, and we have a responsibility to see all the other aspects of calling as acts of faithful discipleship.

> Passions help see us through
> tough times and propel us
> over inevitable obstacles.

Why does our passion matter so much in discerning God's calling? Because no matter what calling you pursue, there are going to be times when it is really difficult. Everything worth pursuing in life is going to have those pieces that are difficult. Marriage can be hard. Parenting can be hard. Every job I know has parts that are hard. If you don't have a driving passion for what you are doing, then you won't be able to endure the hardships for the sake of the call.

In the movie *Amazing Grace* there is a great scene that illustrates this point. William Wilberforce's fiancé challenges him in the midst of a really dark time in his pursuit to end slavery in the British Empire. Wilberforce has gotten sick from traveling and working too hard for the cause. She shakes him out of his despair and proclaims: "You have passion and that matters more!" She was right. Passion mattered for Wilberforce, because the challenges of this freedom movement were great. It's not easy to convince a nation to end a horrific practice that is making powerful people wealthy. Wilberforce stayed with this difficult journey until finally he achieved his goal. Slavery was outlawed near the end of his life. But Wilberforce was relentlessly criticized by the most powerful people in the British Empire throughout his career. Had he lacked the passion to pursue this call through difficult challenges, there is no way of predicting how long slavery would have persisted.

For most people, the difficult parts of their work will be much less dramatic than it was for Wilberforce. Most of us don't face entire nations of politicians who want to ruin us. The hardest parts of my work as university chaplain are short periods of time each year that are not a good fit with my personality. I'm not made to sit at a desk. One of the reasons that I love my work as pastor is that my extroverted personality takes joy from the relationships that I have with students each day. But when summer comes and all of my students go home, I spend as many as forty hours per week sitting at a desk. The monotony of the office work is a bad fit for me. The only way that I can survive those long days in the office is by keeping a key date in mind: the third Friday in August. That is the day the new freshmen arrive for our Christian retreat program. Thoughts of that day keep me pushing through the parts of the work that I don't like. I love the engagement with students so much the rest of the year that it's okay to me that I have those summer weeks sitting at a desk preparing for their return.

Hannah talks about the ways that she struggles when people slip back into addiction or find themselves again living in homelessness. But she has found that the wholistic relationships she is able to build with members of her community help her to keep showing up to work with this population. The relationships are meaningful to her, and it feels like they can make a difference in the things these men and women most need, such as companionship and personal support. The successes and the approach they are taking keep her serving even on the worst days.

CAN WE TRUST OUR PASSION?

There are good reasons why we have been taught to *not* trust our desires. In the Bible, Paul told us that our desire is often corrupted by the depravity of sin (Rom 7:14-25). But often our life callings are driven by our deepest desires, which have been resting in our soul just waiting to come to the surface and awaken our greatest joy.

How would we know if we can trust our desires when making significant decisions? The prophet Jeremiah claims, "The heart is deceitful above all things and beyond cure. Who can understand it?" (Jer 17:9). There have been so many times when I have heard students proclaim that "God has told" them that they should date this person or quit that job. These claims are sometimes just a way of avoiding accountability ("God told me, so who are you to question God?"). But sometimes they are the earnest conviction of a person who cannot tell the difference between God's will and their own selfish desire. If we say that God's calling is often found in the things we most desire, how will we know the difference between our own desires, even our own sinful desires, and the joy that God has placed in our hearts? The answer to this dilemma is found in that same passage from the prophet Jeremiah.

YOUR DESIRE OR GOD'S?

The answer to Jeremiah's rhetorical question, "Who can understand your heart?" is supposed to be obvious. God understands your heart. And more important, God can renew your heart. The promise of the transformed heart that Paul speaks of in Romans 12:1-2 is one of setting right our desires. There is no easy road to recognizing the difference between your improper desire and your rightly formed desire. This takes years of discipleship and a deep understanding of scripture, and even then, the answer may not appear. The most important safeguard along the way is a trusted community of mature disciples, especially a wise mentor, that can help expose your improper desires for ones that desire God. As you begin to pursue your heart's desire, it's a good idea to check in with a mentor before you act on these desires. Mentors can help you get a clearer view in part because they are more objective and unbiased.

If we can get to a place where our desire is formed by the will of God, then our joy is a trustworthy passion to help us understand our calling. A story from my discernment journey is a good example. I vividly remember sitting in one of my accounting classes in undergrad. After class one day when we had received the results of our exams, the professor suggested that I should consider accounting because I was good at it. I laughed at him and said I would be miserable in a life of doing accounting. In retrospect that wasn't a kind thing to say as he was genuinely trying to encourage me. But even then, I knew that accounting wasn't something that I loved to do. I understand the importance of accounting. I can explain how accountants are contributing to God's mission of justice in the world, but I simply don't like doing accounting. I wasn't made to stare at numbers. God had a different plan for me.

At about the same time that my professor was encouraging me to consider accounting, I realized that I absolutely loved studying theology. I had studied the Bible diligently for the five years that I had been a Christian. But in my Pentecostal church, it was rare to study serious theology. I started reading Augustine and Aquinas and Anselm. I could read them all day. I was enamored by questions of sovereignty and the Early Church's figurative reading of scripture. I was also reading a bunch of theologians who followed Paul Tillich. Even though, in the end, Tillich was not convincing or someone I wanted to emulate, I loved reading his books, despite not agreeing with what he said. I was no less thrilled to read Plato, Aristotle, Kant, Hegel, Spinoza, and Heidegger in my philosophy classes. I loved struggling with these big ideas. For many of my friends who were studying business, this all seemed weird and uninteresting. They would much rather just work on financial statements. But God made each of us different, and we had different passions that drove our study.

I went on to pursue master's and Ph.D. degrees in theology, which is a fancy word for the study of God and religious belief. I doubt, however, that my colleagues in school were nearly as surprised as those folks from my Pentecostal church. My college friends knew that I loved studying these books. I know full well that loving theology this way is not the call of every pastor. Some pastors make their way to their calling through social work, teaching, or business leadership. And each of those will influence the way a pastor does his or her work. But I loved theology, and that was an important feature of how I understood my calling to pastor.

For that matter, at the heart of everything I do is my heart and calling to theology. When I parent and when I learn to be a good husband, it is always in a theological key. Decisions about purchasing a car or how to properly observe leisure time are all tinged with theology. But the great part is that my calling to theology never goes away. Theology has become a sort of soundtrack for my life that is always playing in the background no matter what I am doing. That song just keeps playing. This is what I mean when I describe a missional calling; it comes up everywhere when you are doing everything.

Each person has these joys that are an important indicator of calling. Sometimes they start as mere hobbies for photography, music, science, technology, and writing. Eventually a person learns that the expertise that they have built up from years of studying has equipped them to serve the world in important ways. You may have become an expert in computers as you took old ones apart or manage the software to accomplish something new at home. I recently had a student discover a joy in working with persons with disabilities, because a young girl with Down's syndrome had moved in next door to her house. Sometimes these joys are discovered in places you didn't expect.

We also enjoy things in life that may not seem to have any immediate implications for our calling. Many people recognize that they take deep joy in their friendships or their family. Or they may have a seemingly unimportant hobby like fashion or sports. Even those of us who really enjoy our hobbies may not be called to become fashion designers or sportscasters. But passions for your hobbies, for your relationships, or for a certain way of life (urban, rural, etc.) may have a great impact on *how* you live out your calling. My love for sports becomes a way of building rapport and connecting with new people who may not otherwise have a relationship with a pastor. One student recently told me about how her deep love for her friendships had shown her how important it was to her that she work in roles that require community building. So, as you map out your passions, don't limit yourself to the ones with obvious vocational implications (science and literature). Pay attention to all that gives you joy, because that joy is an important indicator of calling.

WHAT MAKES YOU ANGRY?

I suggested earlier that God made us such that every person desires justice. The result of being created this way is a lingering sense that what we see around us is not what God intended. Most people feel overwhelmed by the injustices, the unfairness around them, as if there is nothing they can do. Those injustices you are most attuned to are a significant indicator of God's call on your life.

If you look again at the map that I described in chapter 3, you can easily see that there are needs all over the world. Every X represents a broken country, an abused child, or a threat to our global environment. Of course, there are endlessly more needs than are displayed. Every time I look around, I am floored by the challenges I see. But the good news is that we do not fight injustice alone. Jesus has already promised that a time is coming when the world will be set to rights. All suffering will end as Jesus destroys death, hell, and the grave finally and completely.

In the meantime, you and I have a call to push back the gates of hell as our witness to God's coming Kingdom. Inevitably, we will not succeed completely. I think this realization is the one that paralyzes so many from doing *anything*, because they intuitively know that they can't do *everything*. Don't worry about that. Jesus has already promised that he will set the world to the way it was intended. We are only called to witness to that coming age by our fight for justice in this age.

Not only is Jesus fighting this battle with us, ensuring us that we do not have to end injustice on our own strength, but we are also part of a body that is called to do this work together. I don't have to do it all, because you too are called to fight injustice. Each of the world's needs that are outside of your passion will be the passion of someone else. In those moments when you feel despair at suffering in the world, just know that you are part of a team. You just have to be faithful with your part. I've been encouraged by Hannah's practice of gathering at 5:45 each morning to run with a group of homeless men. I haven't been called to serve this community in the ways that she has. But I am thankful for the good she is doing in the world, and I try to pray for her and her community in the morning when I know that they are out running together.

N. T. Wright uses a great analogy in this regard. He talks about the work of a stonemason who is working on a great cathedral. That craftsman has plans for the stones they are supposed to carve, but they may never know where it will fit in the great cathedral. They just do their work faithfully, and trust that the architect will bring it all together in a work of beauty.

So how do you know which part you are called to work? Where are the needs in the world that most break your heart? What are the needs that make you so angry that you cannot keep yourself from acting? In other words, what are the needs in the world that ignite your *passion*?

Fighting injustice can be incredibly hard. If you try to take on every injustice, you won't be able to sustain engagement for long. But if you fight that injustice that makes you really angry, then you will not stop when the going gets tough. If your heart is broken for hurting people, you will not stop when you are broke, sick, or tired. Roadblocks will become speed bumps.

> Anger and love can be calls
> to action from God.

I think many Christians struggle to think about their anger as a holy thing. There are passages in scripture that tell us not to hold on to our anger. This makes it easy to think that anger is a bad thing. If we hold on to our anger it can make us hateful and bitter, which can lead us to sin and can rob us of love and joy. But anger can also reveal a deep desire for something greater. It can be a call to action. We can be angry because someone's bad choices made us feel unsafe, disrespected, or rejected. We all long for a time when our neighbors care for the people around them and defend them. We hope that others' driving won't make us fear an accident. We want every kid to have food to eat and parents who love them. So the anger we feel when a car cuts us off in traffic or we learn of a child's abuse is actually an indicator of a better world that we all dream about and our Christian faith tells us is coming soon. When we get angry, we should ask ourselves: "What does my anger tell me about God's justice in this situation?"

We can thank God that our Creator has given us a finely tuned meter to indicate when something isn't how it was intended.

When we feel that anger, it will also be important that we don't hold on to it and let it become a seed of bitterness. We may begin to hate the perpetrator of the wrong and cause us to sin. If anger will fuel our passion for our calling, we will need to release the anger as we act on our calling, not on our anger. Sometimes it can be helpful to remember that every person is made in God's image, and each of us has the capacity for beauty, justice, goodness, and anger. We can recognize that often those who commit the greatest injustices on others have themselves been sinned against greatly. Even those who hurt others have also been the victim of sin. Realizing this can help us to release our anger and allow it to focus our energy toward our work of healing and justice.

A LOVING HEART

All that has been said about anger can also be said about a loving heart. Some people's personalities aren't prone to anger, but instead they feel great sadness because of their love for those who don't have all the opportunity that they should have. Their hearts may be broken for victims. Or they may agonize over the broken school system of a nearby poor neighborhood. Like anger, this sadness brought about by love and compassion is an indication of our hope in the world that God has promised, one without death, mourning, crying, or pain.

I've often heard young people say that they are not called to do something because it would affect them very deeply.

College students have told me that they could never work for Child Protective Services because seeing children who have been abused would be too hard to handle. There may be a level of anguish or anxiety that would make this work simply too much to bear. But the sadness a person feels in these situations is precisely what will make them push forward to do excellent work for the sake of those children. You cannot love too much. True, there are healthy and unhealthy kinds of love, just as there is healthy and unhealthy anger. But if we align ourselves with God's love, God's agape love, it will give you strength.

If you will enter a calling that requires regularly facing suffering persons, then you will need to develop some self-care practices that ensure you can cope with seeing suffering. You will need to find ways to better love yourself. God did not call you to this ministry only to be destroyed by it. But the love you feel for those who suffer and the anger you experience when you see injustice are important aspects of how you will do the work day after day.

DISCERNMENT EXERCISE

Take out a piece of old-fashioned paper and a pen and journal for five to ten minutes without stopping. Just write continuously. If you run out of things to say you can just write the prompt sentence again and keep going.

For your journaling, simply complete this sentence: *"Every day for the rest of my life I would love to . . ."*

Now do the same thing, journaling for another five to ten minutes on the sentence: *"I get really angry when . . ."* If anger isn't a feeling you get very often, you may choose to journal with the sentence: *"It breaks my heart when . . ."*

After journaling with each of these questions, write some of the things that you love or make you angry in the "passion" section of your vocation inventory. After you have completed the exercise, find a friend or mentor to read it to. Maybe they can help you see other joys that you didn't think to write about.

TOOLS PART 1:
TALENTS, SPIRITUAL GIFTS, AND RESOURCES

When Joe Sanford took his first Bible course in college, he was already serving as a youth director in his church. He immediately took what he was learning back to the teens in his group and helped open the world of the scriptures to them. With what they were learning, they were able to interpret the Bible for themselves and were empowered to take their faith more seriously. He realized he had a gift for teaching, and it fueled his own passion for studying and learning the Bible. Joe was seeing some of the gifts that would indicate that he would be a great pastor, but he resisted pursuing that calling.

He answered a call to serve as a licensed pastor of a small church while he was attending seminary, though he wasn't certain he wanted to pursue

pastoral ministry long term. Shortly after arriv-
ing he visited a family whose son had just died.
Though he had never met them, he was sitting in
their living room within hours of the death. He realized that pastors had the privilege of being with
people on their worst days (death, divorce, illness,
etc.) and their best days (birth, marriage, new job,
etc.). Joe also learned that his gift to connect with
people made him really good at this work. As a
child, Joe's dad remarked that it was unusual for a
person to have friends that spanned the age spectrum. When he was a teen, he had rich conversations with retired neighbors, young kids down the
street, and his friends' parents. As a pastor he has
been able to use that ability to connect in ways that
lead people to deeper faith.

Joe has been able to see these two tools become vital in serving individuals to deepen their
faith and to see whole groups get excited about
learning. Had Joe chosen to pursue another calling,
God would have used these tools in different ways.
But as a pastor, they have empowered his ministry
to make disciples of Jesus Christ, and he finds that
his work also fulfills some of his greatest passions.

The last major component to pay attention to in discerning
God's calling is also the most complex: your personal toolbox. I use this name—your personal toolbox—to simply indicate that all of us have a unique set of tools that we can use
to minister to the world. Many discussions of calling will ask
you to explore your "gifts." Often this may mean discovering
our spiritual gifts of prophecy, healing, wisdom, leadership, or
other spiritual gifts named in scripture. As we will see, those

are only a part (an important part!) of our calling toolbox. Even while we explore spiritual gifts, our exploration of our personal toolbox will require many more components.

You can't fix the plumbing with a basketball.

You can't fix the plumbing with a basketball. A person can have incredible tools that simply aren't part of the task at hand. If you are someone who is good with a basketball or a hammer, what are you going to be able to do to fix a broken pipe? Not very much. If you want to be a plumber, you have to have the right tools and know how to use them appropriately. Of course, if you are great with a basketball, then that opens up an entirely different set of missional possibilities. When it comes to your personal toolbox, the priority is to understand what tools you have available to you and how you may be able to use them for God's mission.

God's mission is big and broad and in need of workers. There are lots of things to be done. But they don't all require the same set of tools. So we must discern which aspects of God's mission that we have tools to offer to help advance the mission.

THE TOOLBOX

When God calls Moses to lead the people of Israel out of slavery, God asks him a simple question: "What is that in your hand?" This staff that Moses carried day-in and day-out was something he had grown accustomed to. I suppose it's like my iPhone. I don't think much about it, because I carry it every day to do mundane tasks like scheduling, paying bills, and even making phone calls. But this iPhone has also been my pastoral care lifeline when students are experiencing tragedy, and it is my constant connection with my wife—both very holy things to me.

Moses's staff was similar. He had stopped thinking about it. Now God showed him a new way to use that tool to do the good work that God had called him to. The tools that I will introduce in these next three chapters are like that. Many of these things are so familiar to us that we have stopped thinking of them as unique tools that we can utilize for the Kingdom. Here is a quick list of the tools we will explore.

1. Spiritual Gifts / Natural Talents: I'll explain the difference between these two. But what is most important is that you are well equipped with both, as they are both important for vocational discernment.

2. Resources: Your money, intelligence, personal and professional networks, and many other resources help to open doors that would not otherwise be open.

3. Life Experiences: Both good and bad life experiences enable us to serve people and organizations as one that has "been there."

4. Personality: God has made you with a unique way of interacting with the world. This aspect is central to secular career exploration and is often ignored in spiritual discernment.

TALENTS AND GIFTS

As I've explained in previous chapters, what you love to do and the things that stir up strong feelings within you are indicators of God's call on your life. But you still can't fix the plumbing with a basketball, no matter how much you like running water. As a young adult I played on a few different worship teams at my very talented church. I loved playing music. I loved leading worship and participating in worship even more. Many people talked about how passionately I worshiped while playing a guitar (I also worshiped passionately while in the congregation). Later I worked in three different churches as a worship director. In general, my leadership was appreciated. But I was simply never talented enough as a musician or vocalist to spend my life in this ministry. I loved worship. In some ways I was good at it. But I was not talented enough that this could be what God was calling me to do as my primary calling. I still enjoy leading worship. I get to coach and lead my college students as they become worship leaders. In some sense I can even say this was a calling of mine. But I knew that my primary calling was elsewhere.

No matter how passionate or excited we get about something, we are not called to do what we don't have the ability to do. That isn't rocket science. But discovering what we don't have the ability to do can sometimes be heart wrenching.

Sometimes there are needs of the world that also call for abilities that we simply don't possess. I am passionate about the lack of clean water and hygiene for the world's poorest. Our family gives to this cause. I advocate for it with my ministry platform. But I opted not to be a mechanical engineer (my first major when I started college) and thereby excluded my-self from some of the key skills necessary to help provide that water. Both my musical ability as a worship leader as well as the engineering skills needed to collect clean water are skills I *could* develop, but I don't sense that this is God's call on my life.

If you are trying to figure out what to spend your life doing, then the limits of your abilities are a good guide for what you are *not* called to do. Because no matter how well I can drib-ble, pass, or shoot a basketball, those talents won't help me when the sink is leaking. You need the right tool for the job.

Keep in mind that every need in the world is going to re-quire multiple gifts to achieve the mission. To keep with our example, my decision against engineering training does not keep me from giving to or being an advocate for clean wa-ter. I've used the gift of teaching and preaching, as well as my position as a ministry leader, to do that. Water-providing in-stitutions also need fundraisers, marketers, business managers and accountants, educators, web designers, photographers, and on and on.

I hope that by now you are asking, "Then how do I ac-quire these tools to use to work out God's calling on my life?" There are two ways to get these skills.

HOW TO ACQUIRE THE TOOLS YOU NEED

TALENTS

The first kind of skill is what is commonly called a talent. A talent is an ability that is developed over time by hard work and dedicated practice. Talents require a commitment to ex-cellence. Some people seem born with a natural talent for one thing or another, but they still have to develop that talent, or they will never be great. The only way to develop talents is by discipline, like the athlete or musician who repeats a set of skills over and over until they are done with excellence. One essential way to develop talent is by practice. Joe discovered a natural ability to teach the Bible when working with his teens. But then he spent lots of time studying other great teachers to see how they were engaging an audience and began adapting their techniques to a style that worked for him. Even natural talents need to be developed through study and practice.

Some talents are developed by formal education as well. This is the primary way that young people should approach choosing what they study in college. Many students think that choosing their major is the same as choosing a career. But really all we do when we get an education is add tools to our toolbox. If we learn to do accounting, we are not automatically choosing a career as an accountant. But now we will have that tool for any number of financial management roles we may have in future callings.

> Learn competency. Practice
> to use your tools well.

When Joe began studying the Bible in college, he didn't know how God would use him as a teacher and pastor. And he could have used that knowledge in different ways if he had pursued a different calling. Sociology, psychology, theology, math, and chemistry are all tools we can learn and that God can use in a variety of ways. Some tools are more useful than others for the callings you will pursue with your life, so choosing what you will invest your time and energy to learn is an important decision. But choosing what tools you will learn is not the same as choosing the career you will pursue. As you consider your own talents as part of your discernment journey, you should consider the talents you currently have, but you also need to think about the talents you could develop if you trained. There may be some skills that would be difficult for you to learn no matter how much you practice. Some people are just naturally better at math or writing or public speaking. But all of these skills can be improved with practice and training. Often the best way to learn these tools is to get a sense for the ones we can learn most naturally and then to invest our time and energy to learn and practice them.

SPIRITUAL GIFTS

The second kind of skill is what is commonly called a spiritual gift. Spiritual gifts are abilities that can only be given by the Spirit of God and by God's initiation. I cannot teach myself the spiritual gifts of prophecy or healing. If God gives me a spiritual gift, then I can learn to be more proficient at it through practice, but I cannot have it except by God's good grace. There are several ways a person can become aware of his or her spiritual gifts. It's important to study what scripture says about spiritual gifts. There are several lists of spiritual gifts in scripture, including in Romans 12, 1 Corinthians 12–14, and Ephesians 4. Take the time to read those chapters now and you can see the vast array of gifts that God gives. You will notice while reading that the lists are sometimes overlapping but also have different gifts mentioned in various places. There is good reason to believe that none of these lists were meant to be exhaustive, so don't limit yourself to only investigating these. But these are an important place to begin.

Besides studying what scripture says about spiritual gifts, it can often be helpful to take one of the many spiritual gifts assessments that are available. A good free resource is available from The United Methodist Church at http://ee.umc.org/what-we-believe/spiritual-gifts-online-assessment. In just twenty-one quick questions, the assessment will provide a score in each of the nineteen spiritual gifts that are listed in scripture. You can also find out more information about each of these gifts and find some reflection questions that will lead you in developing your gifts further. Whether you choose this assessment or another, talking about the results of your assessment with a mentor will help you to assess whether this gift assessment is helpful for understanding yourself. And your mentor will be able to explain the ways they have seen each of these gifts to be most active in your life.

For most young people, mentors are going to be the best way to understand their spiritual gifts and talents. Joe said that he often thought of his dad's remark that not many people have friends across the age spectrum. That moment of mentoring Joe was a great indicator of a gift that Joe would use later in ministering to others. When you struggle to see what you are good at doing, a mentor can give a lot of insight into gifts you have never seen in yourself. These conversations can also be incredibly encouraging. Most of us like to have someone we respect tell us about the gifts they see in us. Not only does it help us discern calling, but it builds an encouraging relationship with our mentors. Use this discernment journey as your opportunity to ask family, mentors, coaches, and pastors to tell you about the gifts they see in you. Just ask for an intentional meeting to discuss the gifts they have seen in you. Sometimes it can be helpful to start that conversation by using the results of an assessment like the one discussed above.

RESOURCES

Sometimes this area can be the most challenging for young people to think about. By "resource" I mean that everyone has relationships, possessions, and privileges that can be used by God to further God's mission. Taking inventory of these can help you think of new possibilities for your service.

Relationships with people of influence or skill can enable access to ministry that you couldn't do on your own. If you know a person or network of people in a certain industry (law, manufacturing, arts, etc.), then those relationships empower you to access those experts. For example, I know a woman who comes from four generations of pharmacists. And she is rightly considering which of the many areas of running those businesses she would be interested in pursuing. Whether she decides to pursue pharmacy, accounting, management, logistics, or many other careers, she is virtually guaranteed opportunity for work in the businesses that are run by her family and their associates. That is a resource available to her that she cannot ignore. Maybe your parent is a salesperson or a politician and knows lots of influential people in your city or town. Or maybe you have a great relationship with someone who can mentor you in an area in which you'd like to work. These relationships and networks are great ways to pursue opportunities that God may be opening to you.

Sometimes God may use money or other possessions as you pursue God's mission. Your family may own a building that is not currently being utilized. You may own a certain tool or piece of equipment. The old T-shirt press in your uncle's garage may be used to create clothing that advocates for a cause that is important to you. The large kitchen in your home may be able to empower your new catering business. A person of financial wealth can take more financial risks than those with fewer resources and may even be able to fund ministry from their own wealth. Taking inventory of your possessions that may be used for God's mission can be done easily and may inspire ministry ideas you hadn't considered.

You may also consider the privileges that you have as a resource for calling. For example, I have seen how the privileges of my leadership positions have allowed me to speak and advocate for women's leadership in church communities. You may have privileges associated with your race or gender, or you may have opportunities afforded to you as leader of a student organization at your school. All of these privileges can be used by God as well.

DISCERNMENT EXERCISE

Take some time to inventory the skills that you have for ministry to the world. You should make two lists. First, make a list of all the gifts and talents that you know that you are already good at using. This may be high achievement in science, lots of experience in the kitchen, or an uncanny ability to sway another's opinion. In another list, write down all of the skills that you think you could learn, given the time and discipline. These may be something you would study in school or something you could learn if you did it in your job. As I said above, I don't currently know how to drill wells. But I'm confident that I could learn that skill if I work hard to do so. Put those skills in your inventory as well. This is another great area to discuss with a friend or mentor if you are struggling to think of things that you do well.

TOOLS PART 2:
EXPERIENCE

Danielle was a teenager when her mom was diagnosed with breast cancer. The battle was long and painful for her family, and they had enough other challenges that made her mom's illness even more difficult to manage. Danielle was devastated when her mom lost her life during Danielle's senior year of college. She had already decided to pursue a career in nursing as a high school sophomore, but she wasn't really sure why that was the best career for her. As a teenager she knew that she wanted to help people, and nursing seemed like a good way to do that.

While her mom was still alive but continuing to grow more ill, Danielle was offered her first paid position as a student nurse on an oncology unit. She wasn't sure that she'd be able to care for people who were dying of the same disease as her mom, but she soon discovered that serving them was really healing for her, and she felt like she could give back to the people who had served her mom. Because of her experience with her mom, oncology gave Danielle's work a sense of purpose that wasn't there before. She discovered that her experience with the disease combined well with her natural ability as a teacher. She was quickly becoming one of the best educators for new oncology patients. New cancer patients have a lot to learn about their illness, the side effects of their treatments, and how to take on all the new challenges of their daily life. She could speak easily about the pain sensations that come when patients lose their hair to chemotherapy as well as the emotional loss of shaving their head. Sometimes she would even tell her personal story as patients considered how they should tell their children about their diagnosis. The terrible experience of losing her mother as a college student has empowered Danielle for a lifetime of ministry as a nurse. Sometimes people will claim that this terrible thing happened so that a good thing can happen later on. I don't believe that God wanted Danielle's mom to die so that Danielle could have meaningful work. But God used the tragedy of cancer in her family's life to direct and empower her life calling.

Have you ever wondered how God was going to use some horrible experience that you've had in your life? Maybe you knew that some unique aspect of your life was significant for your life calling but haven't been quite sure how that fits into God's plan for you. Or perhaps you've been a victim of a tragedy. While in theory it may not be difficult to understand how these experiences can contribute to your life's vocation, in practice it is often more difficult and can even be a lifelong process.

In the Pentecostal circles where I learned to be faithful, it was common to argue that God calls people to various kinds of ministries *in spite of that person's ability to fulfill that calling.* As I teach about discerning a calling, many people have challenged me with this idea that sometimes God calls people to things they aren't gifted to do. Many have said that God often calls people to do things that they could have never known if God hadn't given clear guidance that stood outside reasonable explanation. "David was a small boy," they say. Jeremiah was too young (Jer 1:6). Peter and John were "unschooled, ordinary men" (Acts 4:13).

Many people mention the story of Moses as a key example of God calling someone in spite of their lack of ability. Moses responded to the Lord's calling by claiming, "Pardon your servant, Lord. I have never been eloquent, neither in the past nor since you have spoken to your servant. I am slow of speech and tongue" (Exod 4:10). They cite Moses's objection as if that's the whole story: "Moses wasn't qualified to fulfill this calling, but God used him anyway." But that isn't the whole story.

Moses had a number of experiences that uniquely enabled him to do the work that God had called him to do. His inability to speak was a minor aspect of what would be required for his calling, even if this minor issue was overwhelming for him. Here are just a few things to consider regarding God's unique preparation for his ministry.

1. The weakness that Moses cites was already completely overcome by his relationship with Aaron. Even if he didn't have the ability to speak well, his brother would be his mouthpiece. The people you know are part of your unique toolbox because they can offer you help in areas where you aren't able to minister. An old friend with graphic design skills may empower you to create a media campaign for a justice issue that is significant to you. Maybe you are networked with a bunch of musicians and bands who you can

call on for a benefit concert. Or maybe your relationship with your pastor will open doors to preach in a neighboring congregation where she has friends.

2. Moving thousands of people across an open desert would be incredibly difficult. While considerably easier, the task wouldn't differ significantly from that of herding Moses's father-in-law's flock. Moving both would require diligence to not leave any behind and an awareness of what would leave them most vulnerable to attack. His unique experience had helped him develop the most basic skills that he would use in this new calling.

3. Moses met his wife while on the run from Pharaoh's soldiers for a murder that he committed. He ended up marrying Zipporah, his wife, because God positioned him in a place to help her family. Jethro gave his daughter in marriage to Moses, gave him work, and supported him with wisdom and advice as he pursued his calling. The people around you who support your calling are one of the many ways God equips you to serve. What unique gifts have they given you?

4. How do you suppose Moses was able to walk right into Pharaoh's court? This would not have been allowed of just any common person. He was only able to do this because of the people he knew from having been in Pharaoh's home. Similarly, Moses's unique upbringing gave him the linguistic skills necessary to speak clearly with both Hebrew people and Egyptian people. His upbringing in a royal home provided him with access that no one else would have enjoyed.

Moses did have some leadership abilities and some learned skills like his language abilities that uniquely qualified him for the leadership role God called him to. But his life experiences were even more important than his talents. His relationship with Pharaoh gave him unique access that was essential to the exodus he led. His relationship with his wife's family and his brother Aaron each supported him to meet his inadequacies through the service of others. Even his heritage as a Hebrew person helped to instill a passion in him for the freedom of his people. It's easy to look at Moses's ability to serve his calling through his own verbal objection to the calling. But a closer inspection reveals that Moses was incredibly well equipped because of his unique life experiences.

Moses sounds a lot like each of us when he issues his objection. He ignores all of the other ways that God has empowered him by looking to his singular weakness that will hinder his leadership. Many of us are prone to look at our weaknesses as proof that we could never do what God has called us to do. All of our other talents and experiences can be ignored because of this thing that we can't do well. God never intends our weaknesses to convince us to pursue something else, something smaller than we are able to pursue. There is no person in the world who can pursue their calling without exposing some of their weaknesses. Our weaknesses are not confirmation to do something else but encouragement to trust others in the body of Christ to do what we are unable to do. Our weaknesses become a place of trust and learning, not a place to turn around and go the other way. Thankfully Moses did not ignore his unique experiences that had empowered him to his calling. But rather, he trusted Aaron to help meet the place where he lacked strength and then leaned into the experiences that empowered his ministry.

Most of these aspects of Moses's life were positive experiences that he was later able to utilize in his calling. But sometimes negative experiences can be used just the same. Danielle's story that opened this chapter is a great example. The loss of her mom was terrible and came at a time in her life that was full of transition and uncertainty. Besides her mom, Danielle had already lost another family member to breast cancer, and two others had been diagnosed with the disease. She had learned that she also carried the genetic markers that meant she was susceptible herself. So even while she was grieving her mom's death, she also feared for her own future and the future of any children she may have. The complex feelings of grief and uncertainty she felt were obvious on the day that she came to tell me that she believed she may be called to a career in oncology nursing. She strongly sensed that this is what she should do, but each interaction with her patients painfully reminded her of her mother's illness. No one would have blamed Danielle if she had simply decided that this path was too difficult. Her life would still have purpose and meaning if she became a nurse in another unit. But she knew that her experiences of loss had empowered her to help others. Even while she feared this decision, she had a firm conviction that it was the right one.

And her experiences have proven to be invaluable to her patients. As mentioned above, she has special insight into the pain and sensation that a patient will experience. And she knows what it is like for a patient to tell their family and friends of their diagnosis. Her experiences of this kind of loss have given her a resolve that is unwavering even while doing a difficult job. And her insight makes her one of the better educators among nurses in her unit. She loves to be the one who administers a patient's first treatment of chemotherapy, because she understands the fear and the questions that arise in that moment. She also understands the holiness of this special moment in a person's life and treats them with compassion and with hope. These special insights have been empowered by her personal experience, which God now uses as a tool for her ministry.

Sometimes God will use your life experiences to empower your calling. Experience will give you a special kind of insight that you use to serve others. But for others, life experience will help them to discover their passions. Danielle discovered through her work that she gets a deep sense of purpose from being with people who are dying. She is honored to walk people toward death with dignity and a sense of hope. Of course, her hope for all her patients is recovery. But when it is clear that a patient will not live, she knows that she will gain a sense of purpose from walking with that person to his or her death.

Whether by equipping you or by helping you discover your passion, God will use your life experiences to craft the ways you respond to God's calling. Whether you have powerfully positive experiences that have given you a vision of what is possible in your work or if you have seen tragedy that has given you special insight into the suffering of others, both positive and negative experiences in your life have the potential to empower your ministry and work.

DISCERNMENT EXERCISE

Spend some time journaling about the most significant changes in your life. For some people this may be a good time to consider writing a spiritual autobiography. There are lots of things that you may want to include in your spiritual autobiography. I suggest you write your story from birth until today with four questions in mind:

1. Where did I encounter God in this part of my story (people, communities, prayer, worship, etc.)?
2. What church(es) was most important in this part of my story?
3. Was this a time of doubt, disobedience, confidence, or devotion to God?
4. Who were the people in this part of my story who clearly knew God?

After you write your spiritual autobiography, go back to your calling inventory and record all of those life experiences and relationships that you believe have given you some unique ability to minister. You may also discover some talents that need to be recorded and some passions that were earlier forgotten.

TOOLS PART 3:
PERSONALITY

Abbey Skrzypczak came to my office during her junior year of college feeling like she wouldn't find her way. She had been studying education and that wasn't a good fit for who she was, so she felt like a failure. After Abbey went through a process very similar to the one described in this book, she discerned that God was calling her to pursue a career in social work. During her training she did internships working with persons who suffer from addictions, and she immediately realized that this was an excellent fit for who God made her to be.

She was initially resistant because she is a deeply passionate and emotional woman. She thought she could never watch people she cared about suffer because it would hurt her heart too much. And her work does break her heart on a regular basis, so she has had to develop some careful practices of self-care. She frequently makes the long commute home in silent meditation in her car. Other times Abbey allows herself to fully feel her sadness and spends time crying alone or with a friend. While she originally thought her emotions would be a liability, she has learned that her heartbreak fuels her passion for the people she serves.

And the people she serves can sense her care for them.

Abbey also recognizes her straightforward personality is exactly what many addicts need. Addicts often spend a lot of time lying and making excuses to family, friends, and employers. Abbey has learned to speak honestly with clients who try that approach with her and to challenge them to be honest about their failures. She is transparent about her own challenges and helps clients see that she isn't setting herself above them or being condescending to them. She knows this is one of her strongest gifts in working with clients.

One of the biggest factors in your satisfaction with your work is the degree to which your personality and your job requirements are a close alignment. This is why personality assessments are one of the most commonly used tools of career counselors. Research has shown that people who have a closer alignment between their work and personality will be less stressed by their responsibilities and will have more joy in their work. While it is true that the complexity of a person cannot be totally reduced to a personality type, assessments are useful because they offer some helpful principles that can offer us a dose of self-knowledge. Every career field and every particular work environment has a unique set of stress factors. Some jobs have constant deadlines that carry high consequences. Others regularly place people in danger of life and health. Others require lots of collaboration or include significant customer service responsibilities. Each kind of stress will affect a person differently based on their unique characteristics.

> Personality is those
> characteristics or
> qualities that form an
> individual's distinctness.

Each career and job also has its own particular joys. For a person who enjoys getting to know new people, a job traveling to new places for training or service would be great fun. But a person who would prefer not to be talking to new people much of the time would never see the joy in this kind of work. Others may love the meticulous work involved with data management or computer programming. Being outside in nature for long periods of time will be freeing for some and miserable for others. Finding work that has regular practices you find enjoyable can be a big factor in how you think of your job. Part of what makes Abbey love her job is that she likes doing something different every day. In her words, "I don't know how people do a job where they are sitting at a desk all day just typing away." Her job allows her to talk with a different client and help solve a different set of problems each day and even each hour. This makes her happier in her work because she has identified some aspects of her personality that align well with the work.

There are also some personality types that are assets to a particular work setting because they suggest you will be a good fit for the job. Abbey is a great example. Her ability to talk straightforwardly to her clients without condescension is a big part of why they are responsive to her. Her personality communicates that she cares about them and that she is being honest with them about what they need to do to move forward. Anna Palmer, who we learned about in chapter 3, uses her authenticity to gain support of clients and business owners. Others may find that their meticulous personality makes them great at administration.

> God uses our
> uniqueness to minister
> in unique ways.

None of this should be surprising. God has created each of us as unique persons and then uses our uniqueness to minister to others. This is part of what Paul indicates when he imagines the hand and the eye of the body of Christ arguing with each other about who is more important. These unique attributes will become a liability in one work environment and will become a strength in another. This is so widely accepted by career counseling professionals that there are lots of tools to help think through how to align your strengths and personality with the work you do.

I will recommend three tools to help you think through your personality and how it may help you in your work. Each of these is a kind of personality assessment. Each one measures slightly different aspects of your personality and gives you a report that describes how you think, act, and relate to the world and people around you. In all three cases you will be required to answer a series of questions about your preferences, and you will provide honest answers in ways that make the most sense for you. None of them are graded in the sense that they don't say that one person is more valuable or important than another. They create categories to describe the ways people think and act, and each category is presumed to be valuable in some way. There are no bad scores on these assessments, just categories that describe how a person thinks and acts.

> Assessments are not
> prescriptions simply
> to be filled.

It's important that you take a healthy approach to the usefulness of the tools. I've seen some young people take assessments like these and take them as a prescription that they have to follow a career path that doesn't otherwise make sense for them. When this happens, the tools become constricting and unhelpful. Despite the fact that the scientific validity of all three of these measures has been challenged, each one is useful in the appropriate context; and each gives a partial view but doesn't—can't—tell the whole story of who you are. As you read results for any of the tools, it's most helpful to ask whether the descriptions they give actually make sense to how you understand yourself. You may ask others you know well, such as your mentors, to discuss them with you as well. If some part doesn't describe you well, you don't need to take that description as truth.

Where the assessments are most helpful is in their ability to create a common vocabulary for you to understand yourself and talk with others. They articulate some aspects of your personality that you may not be able to put into words. When you are talking with others who know these tools and vocabulary, then it gives some language to describe yourself that they will understand as well. This can be valuable with the three tools described here, as they make up some of the most frequently used assessments among career counselors and career development professionals. The other great strength of utilizing these tools is the network of companion resources based on their language. Because so many people have used them, you will find lots of resources to describe next steps if you want to explore or develop the findings further.

MYERS-BRIGGS PERSONALITY ASSESSMENT

There are lots of resources on this tool, as it is a most widely used personality assessment. It is important to note that this tool isn't specifically designed for making career choices or developing skills. And while the latest research suggests that the Myers-Briggs is not a scientifically valid measurement, I still find it helpful in giving some broad strokes to people about how they operate in the workplace.

Each person is measured on four scales, and most Myers-Briggs assessments will indicate how strongly a person's preference is on each of these four scales (some persons may be near the middle of one or more of the scales). The four scales come together to create sixteen personality types. In some ways the sixteen types are more helpful than the four individual scales because there are more resources that help you understand how these four scales interact with one another within a single person. But the sixteen types tend to obscure the strength of your preference for any one of the individual scales. You can learn a lot by looking at each of the scales individually to see how strong your preferences are, and then learning more about your personality type as well. In fact, sometimes when one of your scales is close to neutral, it can be helpful to look at the personality type that's just on the other side of that scale as well.

If you take a Myers-Briggs assessment, what will you learn about yourself? The four scales that the assessment measures are Extroversion-Introversion (E-I), Sensing-Intuitive (S-N), Thinking-Feeling (T-F), and Judging-Perceiving (J-P). The four scales will give you a score for each of the eight traits. The E-I scale indicates whether you prefer relationships with lots of varied people or whether you prefer time with a few close friends. The S-N scale indicates whether you pay more attention to concrete information and details or whether you pay more attention to abstract thinking and imaginative ideas. The T-F scale indicates whether you prefer to make decisions based on rational logic and information or if you primarily consider people's emotions and your own intuition. And the J-P scale describes whether you are highly organized and decisive as you plan your work or whether you are able to improvise and be flexible to emerging opportunities. Each of those eight traits combines to form one of sixteen personality types (ex. ENFP, ISTJ, etc.). As mentioned above, a person who finds themselves near the neutral score on a particular scale may want to learn about both types. For example, a person neutral on the first scale may learn about the ENFP and the INFP and gain insights from both types.

Once you know your personality type, and if what it describes rings true in your experience, you can consult a large resource library about how each one is helpful to your career and your career choice. If any of those resources sound like they are prescribing one set of careers over another, I would strongly suggest that you come back to the idea that these assessments are only as helpful as you find them to be. Don't pursue something that you are quite sure isn't a good fit just because a random researcher thinks it is a good fit based on assessment results. But rather, utilize the insights gained from the resources insofar as they help you name your own traits as strengths and challenges and to understand yourself better.

If you'd like to utilize this assessment, you can get the official MBTI assessment at MBTIonline.com, which will require a fee. You can also take a free version of the assessment at 16personalities.com. The free version is much shorter and will be much less accurate. In my experience, when a person gets untruthful results from one of these shorter unofficial versions of the assessments, they normally can recognize where the assessment has gotten their personality wrong. I have found free versions to be somewhat helpful and the official assessment to be more helpful.

HOLLAND CODE ASSESSMENT

John Holland developed this personality assessment specifically to help people make decisions about their careers. Holland Codes are so widely used that you will find lots of career counseling-oriented resources to help you understand your results.

Holland's theory is based on six personality types that correspond with various work styles and work motivational factors. Each person is scored on all six areas, and then the top two or three types are put in a priority order (highest score is the first letter) to identify a personality type. The six types are Realistic, Investigative, Artistic, Social, Enterprising, and Conventional—sometimes referred to by their acronym, RIASEC. Realistic types are good at working with their hands or with physical tools and machines. Investigative persons like solving problems, researching, and scientific approaches to problem solving. Artistic types may be drawn to traditional arts such as visual art and drama but may extend to other kinds of creativity and independent thinking. Social types highly value personal relationships and are closely associated with "helping" careers such as nursing, teaching, and therapy. Enterprising types are often business or program leaders, salespersons, or those who are drawn to similar ambitious projects. Conventional types are great at creating order and creating systems, and they are often highly detail oriented. After you have taken the assessment you will have a priority order such as SEA or CIE, where the first letter is your primary type with weaker following.

This assessment is incredibly valuable for two reasons.

First, many of the careers that align with each of the types are ones that utilize the skills that come naturally to those with that personality type. People who are working in jobs that align well with their skill set will do better work and enjoy it more, as we explored in chapter 6. Holland Codes for each career are also valuable because we know that when people from a certain type work together, they learn to value one another because they exhibit the same skills and preferences. If you share a personality type with coworkers, you are more likely to be considered good at your work.

Two websites can be important for utilizing Holland personality types. CareerExplorer.com is a free career assessment tool that includes Holland Codes scoring as well as a number of other work domains assessments. Taking the entire assessment will create lots of reports, including what Career Explorer calls your "Trait Report." This report highlights your Holland Codes, which Career Explorer calls your "Broad Interests." There is lots of other information available in this assessment, and you can learn a lot by browsing your reports.

The other important website is ONETonline.org. O*NET was developed by the US Department of Labor and contains information about a large array of jobs. You can utilize the search on that site to find out the daily tasks that a person in that career does, as well as information about education level, job growth, and wage data. O*NET allows you to search for jobs by your Holland Codes, which O*NET calls "Interests." If you decide to do the Career Explorer or another Holland assessment, I highly recommend researching jobs according to Holland Codes on the O*NET site. You can learn a lot about what is required to do the jobs you are interested in pursuing.

Sometimes we make wrong assumptions about a career based on the most visible aspect of that job. But the most visible aspect may not be the most important or the most common aspect of that job. For example, when people think of the work of a pastor, they often equate the job with preaching. But that is only a fraction of a pastor's job, which often consists of much more pastoral counseling, business administration, and program planning than it does preaching. O*NET is helpful because it will help you see what kind of work a job really entails and how job prospects look in the field.

CLIFTONSTRENGTHS ASSESSMENT

CliftonStrengths (also known as StrengthsFinder or Strengths-Quest) is a tool designed to help a person develop their most natural ways of thinking to improve their work. With an hour-long online assessment, participants are scored according to what the tool calls "talents," which is a combination of aspects of their personality, behavior, and patterns of thinking. The result is a list of the participant's top five talents and supplies lots of guidance on how to develop these five talents into "strengths." The assumption is that even though these behaviors and ways of thinking come naturally, if a person invests time to develop these talents further, then they can do that more effectively and deliberately.

The theoretical basis of CliftonStrengths is positive psychology. This is why the assessment doesn't even tell a person their lowest scores. The assumption is that most of us who take assessments like these will immediately look at the areas where we score the lowest and then spend lots of time trying to improve in these areas. The authors acknowledge that if we take a skill that we aren't naturally skilled at and invest lots of effort to improve, we will get better at the task. But even after improving that skill, we still may be pretty poor at it. And likely there is someone who could naturally do that task better than us even after we have improved. There is a cost to all of the work improving a skill that we aren't good at, because we will feel worse about ourselves and be unhappy with the work itself. But if we were to expend that same effort improving a skill that comes more naturally to us, then we can become incredibly good at that task. Now we have a skill we can contribute that can add incredible value to the teams we participate on, and we will enjoy the work a lot more as well. This approach assumes that most workers will spend most of their time as part of a team, and we can learn to rely on teammates for tasks that do not come as naturally to us.

This approach has a good alignment with how Paul describes the body of Christ in 1 Corinthians 12. Each of us does the part that we are most gifted to do while trusting others to also do what God has gifted them to do. There are some limits to this approach that need to be acknowledged. There are some tasks that every person will need to do at a minimum level. For example, even my employees who do not naturally organize their calendar and work well are still expected to turn work in on time, be on time for the meetings, and answer email in a timely way. Even with that limitation, I think the insight that you should spend most of your time developing skills you have a natural affinity for is helpful for young people pursuing their new callings.

CliftonStrengths is available for a minimal fee at Gallup.com

/CliftonStrengths. A very similar assessment can be found at High5test.com. High 5 is a different tool but is also based in positive psychology and gives participants a list of their five most natural ways of thinking and working. So even though it is different, the results look very similar to CliftonStrengths. High 5 has an additional feature that many users will find valuable: peer assessment. Users are able to send an assessment to people they trust and value their opinion and can then compare what their mentors and friends say about them to their self-assessments. I know of no other personality assessment with this feature. Asking for that kind of input can be a great way to enter into further conversation with a mentor or friend about the strengths they see exhibited in you. You can learn a lot by simply taking the results of the assessments into a conversation with them.

YOUR PERSONALITY AND YOUR CALLING

It's important to remember that your personality doesn't determine what kind of work you will do. Many people will be surprised to learn that a large number of pastors are introverts, even though their job requires them to do public speaking and lead groups of people regularly. Similarly, if you aren't naturally inclined to highly detailed work, you may still pursue a career that will require some of these tasks. There are two things you should consider in this regard. First, work that is outside your natural gifting will likely be more tiresome. If it is the only thing you do at work, then you are unlikely to love your work. (But remember, there are things about every job that you won't like or will find annoying.) Even though most jobs will not allow a person to eliminate all of the work that isn't natural for them, finding ways to do more work that aligns with your personality and less that doesn't should be a major goal. The second thing to understand is that your personality may influence the *way* you do your work. You may take an approach to a job that makes best use of that strength.

Abbey is a great example of someone who has altered her way of working with clients, because she knows that one-to-one conversations with them are going to be her greatest tool in helping them to be successful. Other persons in her same job may not have that kind of relationship. They may instead rely on their ability to create a strict regimen of contacts with all of their clients, knowing that regular contact with clients corresponds to positive outcomes. Abbey admitted that she struggles to keep up with administrative tasks. But she has learned to lean into the parts of her work that she knows she does well. Taking the time to understand your personality will go a long way in discerning your calling as well as doing the work well as you pursue it.

DISCERNMENT EXERCISE

Three tools have been described in this chapter. You may also be familiar or know people who are familiar with DiSC, Enneagram, or another similar tool. For this exercise, take two of these kinds of personality assessments. I would highly recommend that one of the two be a tool that includes your Holland Codes since so many of the employment resources are keyed to that tool. But any that we have mentioned in this chapter as

well as others could be your second tool. If you know someone who is familiar with one of these tools, then I would suggest taking that assessment so that you have a conversation
partner. After you have taken two assessments, don't forget to
include any insights you have gained into your vocation inventory sheet.

BRINGING IT ALL
TOGETHER

Joe Garrison started working in student ministry shortly after graduating college. Like most church staff members, he found himself doing lots of different kinds of work as part of his job. He learned a lot about how to write church communications in ways that people would value upcoming programs and they would show up. When he left that job, a pastor from another church recognized Joe's talent in communications and asked him to work part-time managing their church communications. At first Joe took the opportunity as a way to make extra money to support his young family. Before long he had added a couple small businesses and then a couple more churches, each one paying him part-time to manage websites and social media and some of their print communications. Joe recognized that many churches and small businesses didn't have the expertise to create effective communications and were spending too much time doing a poor job of it. He realized he did the work well and could earn a living. He started GarrisonCommunications.com.

After he had found himself in the middle of a successful business, he began to realize that he was also good at interacting with clients and building those relationships. The process of helping them clarify messaging was also leading them to get clarity about their mission. He was doing more than helping them market programs but was helping them know what they were doing in their community and therefore empowering them to do it better. Helping leaders through that process was an important part of his ministry, and it was often this part that was most meaningful to Joe. He has become passionate about helping leaders gain clarity about their work and to communicate that to others. He recognizes that he isn't the one who is improving lives and communities through these ministries. But he is improving the lives of leaders and improving the ministries of church communities by helping them tell a compelling story of who they are to their communities. This is what has given him a sense of purpose.

MORE THAN JUST A PRETTY COVER

If you have gotten this far into a book about discerning God's calling on your life, you are serious about figuring out what God wants from you. This is a powerful time in your life to be pursuing God's calling, and that kind of motivation is important to figuring out what God desires for you. The temptation in this time of growth and commitment is to cut that process short and pursue the first combination of talents, passions, and world needs that come out of this discernment process. It's important that you don't let your excitement or your anxiety about God's calling lead you to cut the process off too soon.

Imagine this scenario with me. You walk into your favorite bookstore or library. You want to read a book and are excited about it. So you go search the shelves and pick just one book that you are going to read. What is the likelihood that you will enjoy the book you choose this way? You may get lucky with a process like this, and you may end up loving the book and tell all your friends about it. But it is much more likely that you will pick a book that doesn't match your interests or requires background knowledge that you have never learned. You begin reading and realize that this wasn't a great choice for you after all. In most cases like this we have done exactly what everyone has told us not to do: we judged a book by its cover! Unfortunately, many people choose their careers this way. We see something that a friend or family member is doing, and the parts we see of that job look interesting enough. But we are "judging a book by its cover" in most of these cases. A great example of this comes anytime I tell someone that I believe they would make a great pastor. Almost every time I tell someone this, their response is some version of whether they could imagine themselves preaching or not. Preaching is a tiny fraction of what a pastor does during the week. But it is the most public and outward-facing role. As a result people decide whether being a pastor is their calling by making a judgment based on a tiny fraction of what a pastor actually does. Many people outside ministry make decisions this way as well: they judge the book by its cover.

Now imagine going into that same bookstore. This time you pull a bunch of books off the shelf and fill a table with the ones that interest you. Once you have a dozen books on the table you begin to read the back covers and maybe the first chapter. You learn a bit more about what the book is about as well as the style of the author. From this deeper understanding of the books you have on hand, you are able to make a better judgment about which ones interest you and which ones have subjects that seem most important to you. What if your vocational journey looked more like this second approach? You could spend some time working to fill out a large set of possibilities for where you may spend your life. Then you do some investigation into the possibilities that each of these callings entails. You pray over each one and meet with a member of your church who does similar work to find out what they do each day and what they love about their work. You look into educational requirements and work opportunities for each one. In some cases you can even begin to work in the field in the way that Joe got hired by a few churches as he was starting his business. Most important, you spend some time understanding how you can contribute to God's redeeming and reconciling work through each of these callings. After having a bit more information, you then begin pursuing the path that seems to fit your gifts, your passions, and God's mission in the world with the closest match. This approach is likely to leave you with two or three great options. This decision may be difficult, but you can know with confidence that all are callings you could pursue with confidence and faithfulness.

This second approach is the one that I hope for everyone who is discerning their calling. Many young people struggle with this slower approach, because they feel the pressure of those who keep asking what they want to study in college or where they want to work after school is done. When you feel this social pressure, you will be tempted to just choose the first thing that makes the least bit of sense for you. Ultimately this approach leads to more doubt and confusion because often you begin pursuing this calling and feel like you have already committed yourself to it. You have taken some classes. You have told your grandparents and your friends that this is what you will do. It feels like you are already committed when you really just aren't sure. You will be in a much better place if you will continue to explore several options until you gain some confidence that you have several good possibilities. Live in the tension of not knowing and allow this time to help you grow in your faith and trust in God.

USING YOUR MAP

Throughout your reading you have been adding lots of tools, passions, and world needs to your inventory. By now you likely understand yourself and God's mission much better. But you may still not know anything more about how you should join God's mission. Now that you have all of this information in one place, the process of filling the range of possible callings will be much easier.

Step 1: Your inventory is divided into three distinct areas. Both the things you love and the things that make you angry make up your passions area. The world and its needs is its own area. And the tools area is made up of your talents, gifts, personality, and life experiences. The first step in discerning possible callings is to find alignments between any *two* areas. For example, you may notice that you have a passion for music, and you are also talented at music, connecting parts of both areas. Sometimes the connections will not be as straightforward as that. For example, I love people and spending time with people. And the world needs people who have deep commitments to their faith and their faith community. My passion for people could certainly be used by God to make me excited about people making deeper commitments to their faith and community. In this first step you should spend some time making as many of these two-point connections as you are able to find and add these to a list.

Step 2: For each of these two-point connections, you will now look to find an alignment with the third area. Don't just look for one set of alignments in this section though. As explained above, at this point you are exploring a whole list of possible alignments that we can explore deeper in our next step. There are three different scenarios that Step 2 may present, each with its own unique requirements for finding that third connection.

Scenario 1: Passion–Need Connections. In this first scenario you have discovered some need in the world that gives you great joy or breaks your heart. Maybe you have learned that you really take joy in mentoring children and have learned about a community of children in need of mentoring. Maybe you are angry about the 800 million people in the world who do not have access to clean water. This need in the world has ignited an anger in you that is strong enough to sustain the challenges of the work. In this first scenario, you are simply trying to discover what talents you have that are needed in this line of work.

The next thing to do would be to survey your tools to see

if you have any unique talents, experiences, or personality traits that would enable you to aid in this work. Answering that question may sometimes require a deeper understanding of the work that is needed. Does this work require people skills, administrative skills, or technical skills? Are there persons who do all of these kinds of work? Though I have a deep passion for providing clean water for those who are without it, I know that there are lots of technical skills required to providing water (collection, filtration, drilling wells, etc.). I don't have any of those skills, but in a different environment I could probably imagine going to school to learn those skills. But I can do something else right now. I have learned administrative, leadership, and financial skills that would make me a good nonprofit leader. I may pursue that calling in the future. I also am a good communicator and talk with many people regularly, which enables me to tell others about the water crisis. And my wife and I earn a good annual income, which enables us to give to water charities each year.

As you can see from my example, when you are passionate about some need in the world, the only question you must ask is whether you have some skill or experience that is useful in meeting that need. Finding some need in the world about which you are passionate is one of the easier scenarios to find your calling because most people have some tool to offer, and most complex needs in the world require lots of different skills to be able to meet the needs. This is why Frederick Buechner's quote has been helpful for so many people: "The place God calls you to is the place where your deep gladness and the world's deep hunger meet" (*Wishful Thinking: A Seeker's ABC*). When you find joy in meeting some need of the world, you can almost always find some way that you can contribute to reconciling that "hunger" back to God.

Key Question for Scenario 1: What tools do I have to make a difference in this need?

Scenario 2: Passion–Tool Connections. This is the most frequent place that many college students begin to pursue their calling. It's not a bad place to start, even though we have seen that it isn't the only place. Those who discover a passion for some tool they have are able to explore a lot of possible needs in the world that this tool enables them to address. In chapter 4 we learned that Jenna had a love and passion for biology that goes far back into her childhood. When she arrived at college, Jenna thought that she would use her love of biology to become a doctor. When her discernment took her on a long path without certainty about the work she would do, she still kept learning more about biology and eventually environmental science. Because she was passionate about science, she knew that any way that she could use that passion to contribute to God's healing in the world would give her life purpose and meaning. This is one of the great gifts of discovering a passion for one of your tools. If you learn to truly love accounting, science, music, or management, then you will find all kinds of needs in the world where you can put that passion to use in healing the world. My experience is that people who find passion in their tools may change the field where they work quite a lot over the course of their lifetime.

Key Question for Scenario 2: What need can I meet with my tools that will give purpose and meaning to my life?

Scenario 3: Tool–Need Connections. In this scenario you have observed a need in the world that you know you are able to meet with your abilities and talents, but it isn't an area that you are particularly passionate about or excited to begin working in. This may be the scenario that is most tempting to pursue without making that last point of connection. Often the need means that there are people who will pay you to do the job. And your tools make you a good candidate for someone who is willing to pay for your skills. But pursuing this kind of work without a passion for it will eventually lead to lots of frustrations. Sometimes this requires that you do the work a little differently so that you find joy in it. For example, one of my pastor friends particularly hates administrative work. She has simply restructured her work so that she has more opportunity for relationships with parishioners in counseling. That part of her work is rewarding, so she doesn't mind the administrative tasks as much. As we learned from Joe's story, this third scenario was how he found his way into his calling. He was good at something people needed. If Joe hadn't discovered a part of the work that he was passionate about, he may not have been able to do the work long term. But he learned that he really loved the client interaction and the impact he was able to have on businesses and ministries as they clarified their mission. In Step 4 I will explain how you can move toward finding and developing each of these areas.

Step 3: In this step, evaluate the list of possible callings that are before you now. It's best that you have six to ten possible callings from which you can choose. If you have only discovered a few alignments, then stay at Step 2, enlisting a mentor to help you with the process. Once you have a list of possible callings you want to explore, you will then begin exploring each of these in greater depth. You can't really research all of them at a deep level at the same time. So which ones should you begin exploring first? Pray about each of these possibilities and discover which of these connections is the most interesting to you. At this point you are not making any long-term decisions. You simply pick two or three of these connections to explore. After you have used Step 4 to explore each of these, you can return to Step 3 to continue exploring other connections. At this point, simply pick the ones that are most interesting to you to proceed with the next step.

Step 4: At this point we know that we are getting close to several possibilities of how we will contribute to God's mission in the world. Each of our three aspects of calling can be discovered and developed further, but each of them looks a little different.

To develop one of our passions, we need education and experience. Beginning to read about a world need or listen to an expert talk about our tools can make us more excited about the possibilities. Often our imaginations are limited by what we have personally seen. Becoming educated about the possibilities and challenges before us allows us to tap into the experiences of others with more expertise. While education will help us access the experiences of others, we also can gain our own experiences by serving with an organization that serves the needs we are exploring. We can be ignited in our passion by learning some additional skills in the areas of our tools, helping us to see the possibility of how that can be used by God to advance God's purposes. One of the best ways to gain the experience is to shadow someone in the field. In some cases, it's possible to intern or volunteer in that field. Whether by your own experience or through learning the experience of others, exposure is the primary way you will discover your passions as well as develop your passions in this area.

To develop one of our tools, we need to be taught through formal or informal education. Taking classes or studying under an expert will help us learn how to use our gifting better and more skillfully. For young people who are still in school, you may choose to study one of your tools in more depth through your coursework. If the tool you are developing is a set of experiences, it's especially important that you spend time learning from experts in that field. For example, struggling with a mental health or medical diagnosis may give some insight in how to minister to others who suffer with that diagnosis, but it would be a mistake to assume that your experience made you qualified to help that person get well. If that same person coupled their experience with the proper training, then they are more empowered to serve that population. For example, we learned about Danielle's experience of losing her mother to breast cancer and how that has helped her to relate to others with that diagnosis. But her experience has been matched by education as a professional nurse, and those two skills together make her much more helpful to persons suffering through breast cancer. No matter which of your tools you want to use to serve the needs of the world, you can always sharpen that tool so that you can do the work better. This can also be an important process for discerning whether it is the best calling to pursue, as you recognize whether you are able to be excellent at the necessary skills.

To develop our interest in one or more of the needs of the world, we will need to learn about what God says about that need as well as what experts in the field are saying about the need. In almost every need that we encounter there will be a field of research and expertise that can help us understand exactly what they need in that situation. Learning from these experts can be done in the classroom or through your own research. We also need to spend time exploring what the Bible and our Christian faith would say about that need. As described in chapter 4, scripture gives us a vision of what God's redeemed and reconciled world is like. Exploring God's calling requires that we study Christian understandings of what a more just world would require.

Trusting God may sometimes require that we let our faith give guidance toward reconciling the needs of the world rather than trusting our own notions of what is best. This is the study of theological ethics, and it can be difficult work. Talking with your pastor or other respected students of God's Word can help to gain more clarity about how the need you are investigating might be transformed by the Gospel. Learning from experts in the field can also grow your interest and passion in meeting the need. The more you understand about it, the more you will be able to envision solutions in which you can play a part.

To develop our passions, we need to invest time and research growing close to the thing that we want to love more. We grow to love a person more as we know their personality and their interests as well as their needs and desires. The same is true of needs in the world and our tools. If we want to love them more, we need to get to know them better and spend more time close to them. If it's a skill, practice it. If it is a community, spend time with the people who live there. If it is an issue of justice, get to know the people and the problems they face better. As you get close to it, your passion will grow. If your passion does not grow for that need or for the tools that God has given you, then this probably is not your area of calling to pursue.

PURSUING POSSIBILITIES

Once you have evaluated some of the intersections of passions, needs, and tools that you have discovered above, it will eventually become time to make some decisions about what you will pursue. These decisions are not permanent ones. Every decision about calling that you make can be changed later, even though some of them will have consequences. For example, if you pursue a degree or training and determine that God has not called you to that field, then you may need to pursue another degree later, but that is not normally a challenge you can't overcome.

> A disciple's path is seldom
> a straight line. Expect
> some detours.

You need to consider several factors in deciding which calling to begin pursuing. Prioritize callings that will include multiple passions or multiple tools that you can employ. The more aspects you are excited about and the more skills of yours that calling utilizes, the better fit it will be for you. But more than anything this decision should be covered in fervent prayer, alone and with your mentors. God may give you clear direction as God led Moses or Abraham. But more likely this will be a decision that you will simply need to make with trust that you have been faithful in your pursuit. When it comes to making this decision, you should make it with confidence that there are no wrong answers to this question. Through the process of this book, you have already limited yourself to only those possibilities that will likely be good choices for you. Choose what you think is best and then begin to pursue it while holding tentatively to the decision you have made. As you take the initial steps toward pursuing your calling, be ready to make adjustments. And know that God will lead as you pursue the calling God has on your life.

DISCERNMENT EXERCISE

Use your calling inventory to make connections between the three areas of missional calling. I would encourage you to find at least ten connections between just two areas. For example, find a passion that aligns with a need in the world. Or find a tool you have that meets a need. Once you have made ten connections of just two areas, use these to make three to five connections of all three areas. Use the description in this chapter on how to do that. This can be another practice that is helpful to do along with a mentor or friend who knows you well. After you have some of these connections between all three calling components (passions, tools, and needs), choose one or two of them that you will begin to explore through research or volunteerism. Keep an open mind as you explore, and remember that all of these are likely good choices! This can now be a fun adventure rather than a decision that causes anxiety and high pressure.

THE UNIQUE CALL TO PROFESSIONAL MINISTRY

Shannon Stringer had just moved across the country and was in an unsettled time of her life when God spoke to her clearly that she should take a position as Christian education director at Bethel United Methodist Church. At the time she only thought she was being called to this particular job, but she soon learned that the skills she had learned as a math teacher also made her a good Bible teacher. She loved helping young people discern their calling and pursue their dreams. So she took one more step toward a calling in professional ministry: she went to seminary.

Shannon says that her primary calling in life is to help people understand the love and forgiveness of God. That started with young people at Bethel and followed her to expanding roles as associate pastor and then to become an ordained elder and senior pastor at United Methodist churches. Most recently she has taken an even broader role as director of leadership development for the United Methodist Indiana Annual Conference. She empowers clergy and laity to do their ministry better by providing resources, mentoring, and training. The thread that runs across all of these various ministries is that Shannon says, "I want to be faithful to what God has laid before me today." Every Christian is called to a lifetime of Christian service, but God has called and gifted Shannon to live out that calling specifically within the life of the church.

One of the most common reactions people have to the content of this book is surprise that God calls people to all kinds of work. As I mentioned above, many people only think about calling with regards to the work of ministers and missionaries. At this point, you should begin to see the breadth of God's calling to all kinds of work. The commitment that all Christians share is faithfulness to the calling of their baptism. For some that will mean resisting evil as a lawyer or accountant, and for others that will mean a ministry of healing as a therapist. But there is something unique about the calling of God to the ministry of pastors and missionaries.

God calls people to all kinds of work.

The clearest explanation of these unique callings is Ephesians 4:11-13. Paul describes a group of callings, not identical but similar enough for our purposes, that can be described together as "equipping ministries." He mentions apostles, prophets, evangelists, pastors, and teachers. Equipping ministries are those that empower the Church to live out her calling. Paul says that these persons "equip [God's] people for works of service, so that the body of Christ may be built up until we all reach unity in the faith and in the knowledge of the Son of God and become mature, attaining to the whole measure of the fullness of Christ" (Eph 4:12-13). This special group of ministers is called to empower all the other ministers and help them fulfill their calling. This is what makes equipping ministries unique: their calling is to help others live into their calling. Every baptized Christian is a minister of the Church, and these equipping ministries are those who help to teach them the Word of God, encourage them in Christian service, and lead them in their work together as a body who loves their community with the love of Christ.

Equipping ministries is a broader term than only those we would typically call "pastor" in a congregation. Those who lead children's ministry, Bible studies, mission teams, youth ministry, music ministry, and a whole host of similar roles would make up this broader idea of equipping ministries. Like Shannon, many people will serve in a number of these different equipping ministries roles during the course of their lifetime. Shannon started by directing ministries to children and youth. Later she became a staff pastor and fulfilled more pastoral responsibilities to the whole congregation. Then she was the lead pastor of a congregation. And her most recent role is equipping pastors and leaders across the state of Indiana in a role with her regional body (Indiana Annual Conference of The UMC). While each role had some unique aspects to it, all of these roles share the lifelong commitment she has made to empower people in their ministries of witness and service.

There is a common set of passions and tools that many of these equipping ministers will share. And discerning whether one has these passions and tools is central to knowing whether God is calling you to an equipping ministry. Some persons will have dramatic call stories where God speaks to them clearly about a call to ministry. Just as we described above, some will experience a direct calling from God that will mean they no longer question whether they are called to this ministry. They will know it is their calling and will only need to decide if they will be obedient to that call. But the vast majority of persons who discern a calling to equipping ministry will not hear God speak from a burning bush or call their name audibly in the dark of the night. Most will discern God's calling through ordinary processes of prayer, mentoring, worship, and submitting themselves to the community's discernment. Much of the rest of this chapter describes some of the passions and tools that a person should look for as they discern this calling.

Prior to discerning these other aspects, there are some prerequisite attributes that a person will need to fulfill this calling. One might think of these traits as akin to the physical fitness test and background checks necessary to become a police officer. Even if someone has all of the other traits needed to be a great police officer, these physical fitness standards and a clean criminal history are entry points to considering the others. Equipping ministries have a similar set of qualifications.

Equipping ministers must be wholly and faithfully devoted to God. A person cannot fulfill these ministries without deep commitment to their faith that guides the decisions of their life. If you do not have wholehearted commitment now, you must work toward that commitment before you can fulfill equipping ministry. As we learned about Shannon in the opening to this chapter, faithfulness to what God has laid before her in the present moment is her primary concern. Without that dedication to God she can't do her work well.

Equipping ministers must have a love for God's Word. Teaching and preaching is not the only task of equipping ministers, and some ministry roles will have more or fewer teaching responsibilities. But I know of virtually no equipping minister who doesn't have at least some responsibility to teach people about the Bible and theology. Equipping ministers need to have a love for the scripture as both an act of personal devotion and the desire to teach it (formally or informally) to others. This is not the same as a calling to preach in all cases. Some equipping ministers only preach rarely, but all of them are called upon to teach about the faith in their various settings. In Shannon's case, her love for teaching is what brought her into ministry work. But the nature of her teaching role has changed a great deal from her Christian education role to weekly preaching as a church pastor to providing trainings at events as she often does now. But that love for God's Word is consistent across a variety of teaching settings.

Equipping ministers must be highly ethical people who are full of integrity. The failure of ministers in this arena has been highly publicized. Certainly no one has every area of sin removed from their life. But every minister must be "going onto perfection" in ways that make it safe to place the trust in them that is often given because of their role. We learned about Joe's ministry in chapter 6. When a family allowed him into their lives just hours after the death of their son, they were placing that trust in him by virtue of his role and authority as pastor. If a person does not have the integrity to accept the trust people place in them, they should not pursue this calling. To see some of the qualifications of equipping ministers from the Bible, you can read Acts 6:3-6, 1 Timothy 3:1-13, and Titus 1:6-9.

If a person knows that they are fully devoted to God, have a love for God's Word, and are living as persons of high ethics, then they may consider whether they have the passions and tools that will empower a ministry that fulfills the need for equipping ministers.

PASSION FOR EQUIPPING MINISTRY

I have already mentioned a love for God and a love for God's Word as necessary passions. But there are lots of passions that may be present in someone called to equipping ministry. It's not necessary that you have all of these passions, but you need to be passionate about enough of these areas that it will keep you going when the challenges of ministry are making life difficult.

You may have a passion for the life of the church. Sometimes this passion is expressed through great love for the church and the rhythms of worship, sacrament, discipleship, and fellowship. If you love to be with your church as often as you can, this may be an indicator of calling. Sometimes this may express itself through negative passions like anger and heartbreak. Sometimes ministers can be extremely angry when local church communities are unfaithful to their calling. If your passion for the church is mostly through a negative feeling toward it, it will be important that you channel that passion toward working for the church's good. It's important for ministers that this passion doesn't lead to cynicism. The Church doesn't need leaders who are mostly angry about Church and who the Church has become. But these negative passions can be an indicator of calling when appropriately channeled.

You may have a passion for seeing persons grow in their faith commitments. Some may get excited about a person making a decision for Christ for the first time. Others may get excited about a small community that is studying the meanings of Paul's letter and the difference they make in their community and families. Because equipping the people of God for their ministries is the primary purpose of this calling, a true joy at seeing persons make those steps of faith is an important aspect of calling. Shannon had been living into her gift as a teacher for a long time before a conversation with her mentor helped her think about the ways this gifting brought her great joy. Much of the reason she loves teaching so much is because of the ways it grows people's faith commitments.

You may already be growing in passion for one of the specialized equipping ministries of the Church. For example, one of my former students pursuing work as an occupational therapist found a calling in a ministry to persons with disabilities. Another young person was a graphic artist and communications person and has found a calling equipping the Church through the communications office of the annual conference. Lots of persons first find their calling to equipping ministry because of a love for children's ministry, youth ministry, or music ministry. As passion grows for any of these specialized ministries, a person may find themselves being called beyond occasional ministry and into dedicated leadership of these ministries.

TOOLS FOR EQUIPPING MINISTRY

There are lots of different personalities that can do this work well. I think many persons compare themselves to the person-alities of the ministers they know and imagine whether they are like that person. Your unique personality will be used by God in how you do ministry. If you are highly organized and make structured decisions, God will use this for ministry. If you are highly flexible and can make decisions quickly and intuitively, this too will be a gift in leadership. If you make friends with every person in the room, then your ministry will look like this as well. If you are much better building slow and deliberate relationships with lots of depth, then these will flourish in ministry work. Shannon long thought that she needed to be a visionary leader if she were to see churches grow, but she learned that her gifting to synthesize what oth-ers were saying allowed her to harvest the visions of others and to articulate a way forward. Her leadership didn't look the same as vision casting of other leaders. But her minis-try has been fruitful with the gifts she already has. In some ways, the diverse roles that a person can take in leadership of ministries can accommodate and utilize the gifts of nearly anyone. The only personality trait that is really necessary for equipping ministry is that you must love people. Maybe you don't love crowds or being in front of people. Nevertheless, there is no escaping the fact that you must still love them. People are the business of equipping ministry. You can't do these ministries without loving them and wanting to commit to them.

Talents are also quite varied for ministry. As we saw with

Shannon, the ability to teach the Bible is a key talent that may indicate a calling to this work. In today's ministry world, talents related to the management of the church can also be a great gift to the church. Managing staff, finances, communications, buildings, real estate, and projects are all part of the work of equipping ministers at times. In The United Methodist Church we consider these administrative tasks to be an aspect of the ministry of Order. A gift to counsel and console people who are hurting is needed in nearly every equipping ministry too.

Life experiences that empower ministry are also quite broad. I often see God calling persons who have been part of a healthy congregation that was pursuing its mission well. Experience in that way of being church enables them to lead other ministries. Sometimes it doesn't require an entire church doing its work well, but just a single pastor or mentor who showed you what it means to be a great minister. Shannon learned the impact of a great teacher when her eleventh-grade math teacher believed in her when others had said, "Girls just don't do math." That teacher's encouragement has planted a firm conviction in Shannon that she must be the one who says yes to people's dreams and encourage their callings. Her experience with her eleventh-grade geometry teacher helped her to see how her work as pastor can make a difference. Often God will use your unique life circumstances to call you into various specialized ministries. Experience with addiction in your family may lead to addiction ministry. Having a disabled sibling may lead to ministry with that population. The examples here are unending, but many people called to specialized ministries will discover their calling this way.

DISCERNING A CALL TO ORDAINED MINISTRY

If a person is pursuing the equipping ministries described here, how would they know if God is calling them to ordained ministry? Ordination is the church's affirmation of a person's calling to full-time and lifelong service to God's Church in ministries of Service, Word, Sacrament, Order, Compassion, and Justice. Some people who are not called to ordination will be called to serve in some of those areas of the life of the Church. God can call a person to lead the church in Compassion and Justice ministries as a social worker or lawyer. God calls people to serve on committees and other ministries of Order for a period of time. Similarly, God will call some persons to ministries of the Word without being ordained. Even a ministry of Sacrament can be extended to a licensed minister while they are serving a congregation. While these various works of lay ministry are important in their own right, ordination is a covenanted commitment of the minister to a lifetime of service in these ministries. It is also the Church's affirmation of the expected usefulness of that minister for a lifetime of service. Those who have felt a calling to the equipping ministries described in this chapter should include discernment about ordained ministry as an aspect of their process. God doesn't call every equipping minister to a lifetime of service in these ministries, but every equipping minister should begin conversations with an ordained minister who can help discern the call to ordination. In its beginning stages this can be as simple as conversations with an ordained minister about your discernment. As you get farther along, there will likely be official processes by which you and the Church will discern ordained ministry together. In The United Methodist Church this is a process that starts at the local church level and proceeds through a District Committee on Ministry and eventually to the Annual Conference Board of Ordained Ministry. It includes lots of conversation and examination by other ministers and laity as well as discernment about whether a person is called to ministry as elder or as a deacon. If you are from another denomination then the process will look a little different, but the minister who is discerning with you should be able to tell you what the process looks like in your church community.

GETTING STARTED

Like the calling to any of the ministries described in this book, a calling to equipping ministry begins as a recognition that you have passions and tools to serve a need that the church has. And like any other calling discernment, some of the first steps in this ministry will include getting involved in an entry level capacity. One of the great parts of doing this in the church is the ease with which you can explore the calling. The church has endless possibilities for volunteer roles of service that the church is always trying to find people to serve. Jumping into any one of those with an eye toward whether God is calling you to equipping ministry is easy to do.

Choose a ministry that interests you and discuss with leaders of that ministry what needs they currently have. Remember that any calling begins with seeing ways that your passions and tools align with needs of the community. Ask leadership what their needs are and describe your interests and skills. Together you can discern a place to get started in a ministry that you may find meaningful. Notice that the alignment of all three of these areas is important. When you discuss the possibility of serving with your leaders, they may be tempted to ask you to do something that is simply their greatest need. And meeting a need is an important part of calling. But you should push a bit in those conversations to make sure you are serving in areas where your tools and passions align with the need.

Many churches need people to serve in worship preparation (ushers, sacristan, room setup, liturgists and prayer leaders, etc.). There are opportunities to lead study or prayer for small groups of various ages. There are often several committees that manage budget, personnel, buildings, mission, and programs for the church. In The United Methodist Church, many of these committees are expected by the *Book of Discipline* to have youth representation. Musical persons may want to volunteer in a choir or band for weekly worship or in smaller group settings for a Bible study or youth group times of singing and prayer. Nearly every outreach ministry of your church will have administrative and planning work that is required to set up for service projects and programs, and these folks will often welcome help with those tasks. The best way to get started is to look around your local church setting for ministry that interests you and then ask your pastor or leaders what needs exist in those areas.

DISCERNMENT EXERCISE

Whether or not you think God may be calling you to equipping ministry, I would encourage anyone to explore their calling inventory map with pastors or leaders from their church.

Schedule a meeting to discuss what you have been discerning. Talk about your passions and tools that you are discovering. And ask what needs exist in your church or community. Your pastor may be one of your greatest assets in discovering ways you can test the various callings that you are exploring. They may have ideas within the church or with community connections. They may also know members of your church who could give you an opportunity to explore some kind of work that you are considering. Don't be afraid to end that meeting with asking your pastor what they can do to help you move toward exploring your next possibilities.

CPSIA information can be obtained
at www.ICGtesting.com
Printed in the USA
LVHW091524100321
681103LV00025B/225